WAY OUT THERE

INSIDE THE JARGON SOCIETY

Late-20th-century America's
most curious cultural outfit
and its Raiders of the Lost Art ...

a recollection by
Tom Patterson

SPUYTEN DUYVIL
New York City

Cover image: Jargon Society staff and officers at James Harold Jennings' roadside art environment near Pinnacle, North Carolina. Left to right, back cover to front: Roger Manley, Whitney Jones, Thomas Meyer, Jonathan Williams, Thorns Craven, Tom Patterson, Jennings (with various of Martha Nelson's Baby Dolls interspersed). Photo by Roger Manley, 1987.

ISBN 978-1-963908-10-7

Library of Congress Control Number: 2024939997

In memory
JW
(1929-2008)

"If you can kill a snake with it, it ain't art."

—dubious assertion attributed to **Lyle Bongé**

1. JARGONIC CONVERGENCE

It was the Jargon Society brought me to Winston-Salem, North Carolina.

J-A-R-G-O-N, anglicized French for "twittering," generally denoting specialized language incomprehensible to the masses. In this case ironically employed as the name of a singular non-profit publisher of writing and art hand-picked by its discerning founder, poet-photographer Jonathan Williams.

Born in the late 1920s, Jonathan was of my parents' generation. I had known him for ten years, and we'd recently begun collaborating on a couple of books, thus inspiring the larger project I was hired to direct from the society's newly opened office in Winston-Salem. I'd spent the last half of my twenties as a magazine journalist and small-press publisher in Atlanta, so the gig was tantamount to a new identity. Not unlike being assigned to the federal witness-protection program.

*

Winston-Salem first caught my attention when mentioned on televised baseball games I watched as a child in the late 1950s. Broadcast commentators like Dizzy Dean and Pee-wee Reese sometimes filled lulls in the on-field action with chatter about the players and their hometowns, so I learned that a few major-leaguers were from Winston-Salem—a town with two names.

And the cigarettes, of course—Winston and Salem, both heavily advertised on TV in those days.

"Winston tastes good like a cigarette should."

"Take a puff, it's springtime!"

Likewise Camel cigarettes: *"I'd walk a mile for a Camel."*

All three brands manufactured in Winston from regionally grown and imported tobaccos.

Winston was the modern industrial boom town that adjoined Salem, a traditional community established by Moravian bishops in the eighteenth century. Separate towns until 1913, when the two were officially merged to form Winston-Salem. After the Second World War the original Salem community was revived as a historic tourist district on the order of Virginia's Colonial Williamsburg.

Also during the early post-war era Winston-Salem established the country's first arts council, after the model of Great Britain's. Spearheaded by men who had survived the war to prosper in its wake—the affluent sons of great white industrialist fathers—these efforts sought to establish an identity for the city as an enlightened place that honored its heritage and appreciated the arts.

I was a teenager in the mid-1960s when I first heard about the North Carolina School of the Arts, the only state-supported arts school in the country, newly opened in Winston-Salem. A piano prodigy from my Georgia hometown won a scholarship to study there. He must have been in his senior year at the school when I first visited Winston-Salem in 1971, as a college dropout passing through while hitchhiking to New York. I spent a night on his living-room sofa next to the baby grand piano. It was autumn, and I awoke to a stunning view of the city's skyline emerging from a canopy of fiery leaves.

Winston-Salem looked like it might be a cool place to live.

*

In an era when North Carolina promoted itself as the State of the Arts, Winston-Salem was often known as the City of the Arts. And the city's leading arts cheerleader was R. Philip Hanes Jr., the retired CEO of Hanes Dye and Finishing Company, a branch of the locally based Hanes textile empire. A mover and shaker on the national culture scene, he had emerged as Winston-Salem's unofficial arts p.r. agent by the time I was getting acquainted with the city. A Yale grad whose father bankrolled the restoration of Old Salem, Philip was a founding patron of the School of the Arts, and a staunch supporter of local and regional culture.

The Jargon Society was one of the lesser-known causes Philip championed. He and Jonathan Williams were in the same age bracket and had known each other for twenty years. Philip was a key figure on Jargon's board of directors. His eclectic art tastes extended from the Italian Renaissance and the American Ashcan School to vintage psychedelic rock-concert posters. He had a soft spot for fringe culture, and he enjoyed tweaking the nose of the establishment he and his family represented. He delighted in fraternizing with avant-garde writers and artists, and he was on friendly terms with the Beats and the Black Mountain poets. Hence his affinity for Jonathan, a gay Ivy-League dropout who spent a couple of years at the notoriously artsy Black Mountain College.

At Black Mountain Jonathan had published several of the most important early Jargon titles, by writers including Robert Creeley, Henry Miller, Charles Olson, and Kenneth Patchen. Still active almost thirty years after the college closed, the Jargon Society was in effect Black Mountain's last institutional vestige.

*

Jonathan Williams grew up and attended prep school in Washington, D.C., but his roots were in Appalachia. The only child of southern parents, he was born in Asheville, and his main residence since his Black Mountain days was the North Carolina house where the Williams family moved in the 1940s. Skywinding Farm, his father T. Ben Williams named the place—forty hillside acres in the Nantahala Mountains, near the jumping-off point to northeast Georgia, James Dickey's *Deliverance* Country.

By the early 1980s Jonathan's father was long deceased, and his aging mother Georgette spent the winters in Winston-Salem. During frequent visits to the twin city Jonathan had gotten to know Philip Hanes and a number of other Winstonians who shared his interests and helped support his idiosyncratic cultural endeavors.

JW was supremely confident, opinionated, charismatic, and persuasive. Typically dressed in tweeds, he was upwards of six feet tall. He smoked fragrant cigars, drank high-grade whiskey, and spoke in a deep, authoritative voice that commanded attention and respect, not to mention amusement, as he was also a natural comedian. Like a good general in an army of bright eccentrics, he was effective in marshaling his troops, and he had cut a swath through Winston-Salem's art community, cherry-picking its most aesthetically astute exponents.

Other locals Jonathan had enlisted in the Jargon cause were Doug Lewis, headmaster of a well-regarded private academy known as the Summit School, and Ted Potter, director of the Southeastern Center for Contemporary Art, aka SECCA, which occupied one of the former Hanes family houses in northwest Winston. Both were members of Jargon's board.

My former college English professor Whitney Jones had moved to Winston in 1977 to launch a new career as a fundraising consultant. A Black Mountain enthusiast and informal promoter of the school's legacy, he had signed on as Jargon's volunteer president, and his first wife Robyn became the society's secretary for several years.

The treasurer, likewise an unpaid volunteer, was Thorns Craven, director of Winston-Salem's Legal Aid Society. Jonathan had recruited him after learning he was a fellow Thelonious Monk fan—testament enough to his aesthetic acuity. Like Whitney, Thorns was in his early forties, my senior by a decade.

The only paid positions at the Jargon Society had been those of Jonathan and his partner, fellow poet Thomas Meyer, who split a $20,000 annual director's salary between them. Then, at the society's annual board meeting in January 1984, I was hired to direct Jargon's Southern Visionary Folk Art Preservation Project, and simultaneously promoted to become the society's nominal executive director.   I hadn't applied for this hybrid position, but there it was, and there was nothing to say but yeah!

Although I would officially be performing two jobs, it was understood to be a three-year, half-time position, paying $10,000 yearly with health-insurance benefits. Jonathan was effectively kicked upstairs to assume the title of Publisher, formalizing the role he'd filled ever since he founded the Jargon Press.

*

I hadn't expected a salaried position. Jonathan and I had been talking about his offer to publish two books I was writing, extended profiles of Eddie Owens Martin (aka Saint EOM) and Howard Finster. Both of these larger-than-life southern characters had turned their rural yards into elaborate, world-class art environments, which we aimed to showcase in color photographs in the two books. Meanwhile, Jonathan was working on a book of short-form, photo-illustrated texts about artists, art environments, and other people and places that held special interest for him in his native region. He referred to this collection of essays, poems, photographs, and extended captions as his *Big Book of Southern Folk Art,* alternately known as *Way Out People Way Out There.*

In brainstorming about how to raise funds for the three books, we decided to emphasize the preservation angle—an obvious concern with places like Pasaquan and Finster's Paradise Garden. And we conjured the idea of a special project for these and other related purposes.

Voilà le Southern Visionary Folk Art Project! The Folk Art Project, as we informally called it.

It was an ambitious undertaking—a commitment to document the work of visionary folk artists throughout the region, assemble a collection, and explore the possibilities of a museum devoted to the work, all within a three-year time frame. Our preservation advocacy mainly consisted of throwing a spotlight on art sites like EOM's and Finster's.

We applied the hybrid term "visionary folk art" to distinguish our focus from folk art as conventionally defined—objects handmade according to traditions passed down through generations. Our interest was art made by autonomous, vernacular creators impelled by personal, visionary sensibilities—quite a different thing, and one we knew when we saw it, especially when it spilled out into the artists' yards to form traffic-stopping environments. Preliminary investigations had revealed many such artists working in the American South, our native region. Some of them—EOM and Finster included—claimed to have literally beheld visions akin to those reported by the biblical prophets.

There were maybe 100 people in the United States who took a serious interest in such things, but that was about to change. The field of visionary folk art, self-taught art, outsider art, or whatever you wanted to call it would soon become a very big deal.

Visionary art was of course a timeless phenomenon, as old as human history. The southern vernacular variant on this eternal aesthetic strain certainly wasn't new either. For years Jonathan had been photographing examples in the American South and other parts of the world. He'd talked to the artists who were still alive and had written down bits of their conversation that caught his poet's ear.

I had maintained a personal interest since my southern childhood. I was six in 1958, when I first beheld Stephen Sykes' massive junk-sculpture temple on the outskirts of Aberdeen, Mississippi—*Incuriosity House*, Mr. Sykes called it. It was a revelatory experience that sharpened my eye for anything remotely like it—any kind of unusual yard decoration and anything that looked handmade to suit an individual's personal vision and imagination.

Flash forward to Laurinburg, North Carolina, 1974, and my first meeting with Jonathan Williams. I was an English major approaching graduation at St. Andrews College, where Jonathan was a visiting writer that spring. Among his other distinctions he was the first person I'd ever met who shared my enthusiasm for these idiosyncratic yard displays. We didn't have a catch-all name for the phenomenon, but specific examples became a subject of ongoing discussion. I also shared Jonathan's interests in poetry—which I sometimes wrote—and jazz.

In 1980 JW and I visited Pasaquan and Paradise Garden—the first time for me in both cases. The rest followed from those revelatory experiences, and from my contemporaneous friendship with Atlanta art dealer Judith Alexander, who became a mentor and, for a brief interval, my part-time employer. During my Atlanta years

Judith introduced me to the work of other self-taught, visionary artists—Bill Traylor, Nellie Mae Rowe, Mose Tolliver, Georgia Blizzard, and Juanita Rogers, among others.

My eyes began to open wider.

*

The move to North Carolina marked a major personal transition. Not only was I taking on a new job and a new identity of sorts, but I was also newly separated from Ellen, my wife of four years and companion of the last seven—poet and big-bank office worker. Having found our lives running in incompatible directions, we'd parted company and would formally divorce a few months after I left Atlanta, although we maintained an enduring friendship.

On arriving in Winston-Salem I moved into a comfortably furnished, two-story house overlooking the Washington Park ravine. I'd leased it for six weeks from resident owner Bob Knott, an art professor at Wake Forest University, while he was vacationing with his family in New England. The house was seventy years old, a sprawling, barn-shaped bungalow with a basement where I was able to temporarily store my belongings.

I enjoyed having the premises entirely to myself. The west-facing front porch was so high above the street, and so secluded by densely foliated trees and shrubs on either side, that I could sit out there in the mornings unobserved, naked except for my glasses while I sipped my first coffee. On weekday mornings I typically threw on a t-shirt, athletic shorts, and sneakers, and ran for half an hour along the nearby streets and park trails. My half-time employment status left me unconcerned about getting to my desk early.

The Jargon Society's corner office at 1000 West Fifth Street, in the city's West End, had originally been the dining room of a two-story, Tudor-style house from circa 1920. The second-floor offices, originally bedrooms, were shared by Whitney Jones' fundraising business and a word-processing company called Wordsworth.

Entered through French doors from the foyer on the ground-floor, the Jargon office was equipped with an antique desk, a telephone, and a fancy electric typewriter, and otherwise furnished with dark, wooden shelves and tables for displaying Jargon books. In a room of about twelve-by-twelve feet, most of the wall space and about half of the surface space was occupied by art Jonathan had collected, including paintings by Finster, painted concrete face masks by Saint EOM, and a mud-caked cow-bone sculpture by Juanita Rogers.

Standing out from all the funky folk art was a more slickly sophisticated sculpture—North Carolina artist Jerry Noe's *Neon Rock*, a plugged-in Plexiglas vitrine containing a slab of ersatz grass on which a heavy chunk of solid, natural stone was outlined with a slender tube of glowing orange neon.

2. NEW IN TOWN

To begin building a new social life I attended art-show openings at SECCA and a handful of other local venues. An artists co-operative called Artworks had started a gallery on Sixth Street downtown, where a new show premiered on the first Friday of every month. Other artists rented private studios and personal exhibition spaces in nearby buildings, and they likewise opened their doors for those first-Friday events.

It was also easy to meet people at the small businesses near the Jargon office, along the ridge-top where Fourth Street intersected with Summit Street and Brookstown Avenue. The neighborhood was a nexus of locally owned shops and bars or dining establishments, notably Rainbow News and Cafe´, Johanna Shober's bar and bistro, the Zevely House restaurant, and the West End Cafe—places where people gathered and mingled all afternoon and into the evening.

My office occupied a seemingly special location at the western terminus of Four and a Half Street, which I could see out my office window. Making an uphill beeline for downtown, it ran halfway between Fourth and Fifth streets for a distance of four long blocks. In days of yore when the stately homes along the two outlying streets were still standing and occupied by the city's gentry, Four and a Half Street was lined with the small homes of their African American servants—all long gone by the 1980s.

*

About 125 miles to the southeast, in the Carolina Sandhills, was St. Andrews, where I earned an undergraduate degree in English. Several friends and associates I knew there had landed in the Winston-Salem area. Deborah Coffin, for instance, I'd met during her freshman year, after I graduated. Picture a darker-haired Hayley Mills. During her first semester she fell hard for Randy Kauffman, a quiet, brilliant science major whom she married. They were a cute couple, and still students when they had their two children—son Berkeley, born in 1976, and daughter Rebecca, two years later.

After he and Deb graduated—her degree was in philosophy—Randy was hired as research-and-development director at a glass-decorating company in High Point, North Carolina. A few years later they were divorced, and by 1984 they maintained separate houses. Randy lived in Winston-Salem, and the children came and went according to a mutual custody-sharing arrangement. Deb's house in High Point was twenty miles from me, mostly on a four-lane highway that she traveled several times a month in order to transport the kids.

Deb and I connected by phone, and soon we were spending a lot of our time together. I made fast friends with Berkeley and Becca—then eight and six years old—and the four of us enjoyed a few memorable field trips. I also met Deb's friends, mostly artists who lived in nearby Greensboro, the third city of North Carolina's Piedmont Triad.

Then there were Deb's younger siblings Linda and Danny. The three of them had grown up in Cincinnati, and as far as I could tell, the only reason Linda and Danny were in High Point was because Deb had moved there first. They had their own houses, but they seemed emotionally dependent on their elder sister.

The name High Point definitely rang ironic. Granted, John Coltrane spent his childhood there, and its appellation identified it as a high-altitude spot on the railroad through the middle of town, but it was a less-than-spectacular place. Except for a few older, tree-lined neighborhoods including Deb's, it was a drab-looking burg with a dead, treeless downtown district. The only thing going for it was the international furniture market that transformed it into a livelier city for one week every spring and another week in the fall.

When Deb and I started seeing each other she worked part-time waiting tables at Market Square, a restaurant in a spruced-up factory building. It seemed to be one of the few downtown businesses that brought people in throughout the year, but of course it was especially busy during the twice-yearly furniture-market frenzy.

I had hardly seen Deb since her early days at St. Andrews, when she was still in her teens and still known as Debbie. She was a different person when we got reacquainted—in her late twenties, a single mother of two very bright, incredibly cute, inquisitive children whom she clearly adored.

Deb told spellbinding stories about her own childhood and her complicated family. Because she was button-cute, super-smart, and charismatic, she was crushed on by everyone who knew her, male and female. Her German friends Dieter Elwert and Uli Schemp—first cousins from a wealthy European industrial family—were besmitten. There was some mutual heat between her and a handsome redneck silent-Sam type name of Mike Turner. And then there was the charmingly chatty British guy named Bev Horlick, who made no secret of lusting after Deb. Far was it from me to intrude on any of those relationships, but I suppose I did, a little, for a few months.

My car was a 1980 Honda Civic, dark brown, with a souvenir bumper sticker from Pawley's Island, South Carolina, plastered onto the hatchback. "ARROGANTLY SHABBY," it announced.

Deb drove a white VW bug with the phrase BRUTAL HOSTESS emblazoned across the back in big, black, stick-on letters. It sounded like the name of an s-&-m catering service, but in fact it was an in-joke she shared with a few local friends—a fictional punk-rock band in a novel allegedly being written by one Chuck Alston, aka Also Aswell.

Chuck was a Greensboro artist and character who founded a group of likeminded weirdos he named the Cosmic Ray Deflection Society of North America. Loud and lovable, with natural pale-blond hair matching Andy Warhol's wig, he seemed to fancy himself a kind of southern Ken Kesey. Instead of a psychedelic bus, he drove a profusely decorated station wagon he called the Cosmic Raymobile.

*

Meanwhile, back in Winston-Salem, after the Knotts returned to their home in Washington Park I settled into a small apartment on Sunset Drive, in a house overlooking the hillside homes of the city's West End, just across the east-west corridor of Interstate 40. Entry to my new place was through a box-shaped, single-story addition tacked onto the back side of the sixty-year old, two-story house. The downstairs rooms in the back of the original house were also part of my unit, with higher ceilings than the add-on box, which contained a tiny kitchen, a bathroom, and a cramped, shag-carpeted living room.

A gravel driveway curved around behind two houses on the south side to access my scrubby little yard and an unpaved parking area, beyond which was a steep, densely wooded ravine with a narrow stream running through the bottom. The absentee owner was an airline pilot who rented the rear apartment to me for $275 a month. The larger, two-story apartment in the front of the original house went for $400 a month.

The house's subdivision was such that the front apartment's kitchen backed up to a wide closet in my bedroom. The young women who lived in the front apartment when I moved in had a small, long-haired dog—a terrier or a Pekingese or something—that was prone to yip-yap for hours when its biped housemates weren't at home. The dog always sounded like he was in their kitchen, if not trapped inside my bedroom closet.

Fed up with the racket, about three weeks after I moved in I left a polite note on the neighbors' front door with a request that they do something about their dog's incessant barking while they were away. Days later, with no reply to my note and no change in the dog's habits, I decided to retaliate.

One evening when I knew the neighbors were home—I could hear their muffled voices, and the dog wasn't barking—I put on the most aggressively grating, obnoxious record I owned, an LP by James White and the Blacks, and turned the volume all the way UP.

Then I left my apartment, locked the door, got into my car, and drove away.

3. LET'S PUT ON A SHOW

Within days of transplanting myself from Atlanta I set up a meeting with Roger Manley, whose acquaintance I'd made in 1983 at a folk-art conference in DC. A bear-sized figure with a ruddy complexion, reddish-blonde Brillo hair, and an Amish-style beard with no mustache, Roger was a folklorist and photographer living in Durham—a contemporary who knew more than anyone else about visionary folk art in North Carolina. We paid mutual visits and spent some time on the road together, traveling to see artists including Raymond Coins and Vollis Simpson.

Coins was a farmer living in the foothills north of Winston-Salem, and a master of reductive carving. He created stele-like, stone relief tablets and in-the-round figures with bulbous heads and inscrutable faces. Simpson built the world's largest whirligigs—huge, wind-powered assemblages with hundreds of moving, scrap-metal parts—and installed them on his rural property at a five-points intersection near Wilson, North Carolina. "Acid Park," local kids had nicknamed it, for easily imaginable reasons.

Those first road trips with Roger were limited to sites well inland from the Atlantic coast, but the artist to whom Roger was clearly most devoted—ninety-year-old

Annie Hooper—lived on the Outer Banks. He told me a lot about her and showed me his evocative photographs of her standing in her house, surrounded by scores of her gnarly-looking driftwood figures.

Roger's chance meeting with this pallid, diminutive woman during a disappointing first semester of college had marked his introduction to the realm of visionary folk art. In the months before I moved to North Carolina he was networking with the Jargon Society on Mrs. Hooper's behalf. He and Jonathan had secured a small foundation grant to inventory her biblical sculptures and interview her at length about her life and her art.

In addition to his groundbreaking documentary work on the self-taught artists he'd been tracking since the mid-1970s, Roger had amassed striking works by a number of them. It wasn't a collection strictly speaking, since most of these pieces had been given to him or acquired through trading, but together they made a strong impression in his small millworkers' cottage in East Durham.

Before the summer was over Roger introduced me to veteran collector Robert Lynch, an urbane, gay, intellectual, African American/Native American attorney and unpublished poet, recently returned to his family farm in rural Halifax County after a decade of self-exile in New York. A fascinating, complex individual, he became a friend and a valued ally in our project. His collecting had been consistently focused in his home region of northeastern North Carolina, the state's most economically impoverished corner. Despite its deprived status, the area proved fertile ground for Robert's explorations. He'd found several remarkable but largely unknown artists working within fifty miles of his home, including Leroy Person, Vernon Burwell, Jeff Williams, and QJ Stephenson. All were African Americans except for Stephenson—"my white boy," Lynch, with a sly grin, called him.

My first big initiative for Jargon's Folk Art Project was an exhibition to showcase some of the art that interested us. I enlisted Roger as my co-curator. It was a major undertaking, considering our mutual novice status and the abbreviated timeline. Not knowing any better, we committed to showing works by twenty artists from all over the American South in an exhibition to open in early January 1985. This gave us five months to pull the whole thing together.

I found a site for the exhibition in one of the galleries at the Sawtooth Center for Visual Art, a reconditioned hosiery factory in the middle of downtown Winston-Salem. The original building had been augmented with modern additions to house art classrooms, a theater, a restaurant, meeting rooms, and three galleries. I had to present a formal proposal to the center and to the city's

Arts Council, which oversaw the galleries.

Jumping through those hoops gained us the use of the R.J. Reynolds Gallery, an awkwardly configured space below street level, with an adjoining storage room where we were allowed to stash the works as they came in. I scheduled a reception for the last weekend in January, to coincide with the Jargon Society's annual board meeting, for which I booked the Sawtooth Center's banquet room. We would install the exhibition earlier in the month.

*

Roger and I had just started planning the show when Deb's friend and neighbor Amanda Winecoff introduced me to James Harold Jennings, a remarkable individual who had thus far escaped Roger's visionary-art radar.

Amanda was a weaver and her husband Jim a wood craftsman, and some of their colleagues lived in the rural foothills north of Winston-Salem. On her way home from that area one day, Amanda had taken an unfamiliar short cut. Before she reconnected with familiar highways she happened to pass a display of painted wooden figures and miniature buildings out in a field by the road, as she described the scene to me shortly thereafter. Of course I wanted to investigate immediately.

Amanda said she couldn't describe or map the route, but she was sure she could find the place again. So we all squeezed into my little Honda—Amanda, Deb, Berkeley,

Becca, and me—and I drove us north on US 52 to the King/Tobaccoville exit, where the monadnock dome of Pilot Mountain loomed in front of us. From the exit Amanda directed us along several miles of rural blacktop until we reached the destination on the right side of a sharp curve south of Pinnacle.

Sure enough, there was a patch of high weeds you could call a field, distinguished by a group of sculptures, very small wooden buildings, and propellor-equipped wind toys on tall, spindly poles—all made from sawed-off, cut-out bits of found wood and scrap lumber painted in a curious mix of bold colors and drab pastels. I pulled the car over in a dirt clearing at the edge of the road.

As we exited there emerged from one of the tiny buildings a wiry, gnomelike figure dressed in shades of brown including a knit toboggan cap, with what looked like homemade tool belts and paintbrush holders strapped around his torso. Directly over his heart, on the front of his chest, was a leather-encased portable radio playing mountain string-band music from the local station in nearby Mount Airy.

Obviously nervous, he turned the radio volume down and greeted us shyly, then we introduced ourselves. He told us his name and shook my hand tentatively, as if unaccustomed to the gesture. His bony hands were freckled and paint-spattered.

"Some people call me James, and some calls me Harold, and some of 'em call me James Harold."

We spent a couple of hours with him. The images he'd rendered in painted, cutout wood scraps included birds, snakes, four-legged animals, and rudimentary humanoid figures, some of which sprouted wings and wore white gowns. There was a lot of loose, geometric-abstract patterning and stylized celestial imagery—sunbursts, crescent moons, and five-pointed stars—and several brightly painted airplanes with propellors spinning in the wind.

The most elaborate piece with moving parts was a model Ferris wheel nearly six feet tall. Painted in pastel shades with candy-red accents, it was equipped with individually constructed gondola seats occupied by cutout cartoon figures, and a central apparatus that allowed it to slowly turn with a light push.

One of the small, slapdash buildings seemed to function as Jennings' studio, where he could stand in one spot—there was no room to sit—and reach any of the tools, brushes, and paint cans stored in the myriad shelves, cubbyholes, and niches he'd built into the interior walls. The cubicle was too small to accommodate more than one person at a time.

On a bluff across the road was the weatherbeaten Victorian farmhouse where Jennings had been raised and lived alone ever since the death of his schoolteacher mother. He led us onto the front porch and showed us the interior, which was mostly empty except for his bedroom on the top floor, where a window in the front roof gable gave him a bird's-eye view of his roadside constructions. The only furniture in the room was the narrow cot on which he presumably slept at night. Much of the surrounding floor space was occupied by neat stacks of old *National Geographic* and *Popular Mechanics* magazines and a set of well-thumbed encyclopedias.

In the high weeds surrounding the house Jennings showed us the remnants of huts and hideaways he'd built years earlier, before he moved his curious operation down the hill and across the road. Strewn on the ground I found several small items he'd made and painted much earlier and evidently forgotten—sun-faded windmill gizmos with the paint peeling off and a scrap-metal slab with the hand-painted admonition "NO HUNTING."

From his timid behavior I got the impression Jennings wasn't accustomed to visitors. By the time he'd spent an hour showing us around he had warmed up to us, and he didn't seem to mind answering the questions I put to him. He said he was born in 1931 and had lived there all his life. His mother left the fifty-acre tobacco farm to him when she died in 1969, and he hadn't cut his hair since then.

When Deb asked to see his hair he removed his brown toboggan cap, and the wavy tresses fell down from his head all the way to his waist. The closer-growing hair covering the top of his head was gray, but it was dark red from just below his ears.

Berkeley and Becca were mesmerized. Berkeley asked a question or two, but mostly they kept quiet as they watched Jennings, taking it all in with their wide eyes.

As we walked back across the road to the site of his newer work in progress, I inquired about Jennings' materials. He said he collected scrap wood wherever he found it, and he bought old cans of paint at a discount from the hardware store in Pinnacle.

"The labels come off, so they sell it cheap, and I don't know what color it is till I bring it back here and open it."

He showed us the bicycle he rode into Pinnacle and anywhere else he needed to go. He'd given up driving a car years ago on account of his nerves, he told us.

When I asked where he got ideas for his art, he said, "From the dictionary and words I find in there. Like *psychokinesis* and *metempsychosis*." Pronounced "psspsycho-kinesis" and "medium-psychosis."

He described the brightly pulsating patterns he saw when he closed his eyes and pressed his eyelids with his fingertips.

"Sometimes I get ideas from lookin' at them designs."

I inquired if he ever sold any of his things, and he said yes, then he named prices for a few items—ridiculously low, ranging from three to fifteen dollars. I told him they were underpriced, then I bought several. I mentioned the exhibition Roger and I were organizing and asked if we could put some of his pieces in the show. He said he'd never had any of his things in an art show.

"We can sell them for you if you'd like us to, but we'll set higher prices for them. You're practically giving them away. There are people out there who'll gladly pay more."

He eyed me intently and seemed to be evaluating what I was saying.

I picked out about ten pieces, more than we had room to carry along with the five of us in my compact car. Deb bought the best piece—a thick, coiled vine about six feet long, minimally carved and elaborately painted to resemble a python or boa constrictor. I think she paid something like twelve dollars for it. We carried what we could accommodate in the already-crowded car, and I promised to return in a few days to pick up the other pieces.

Jennings turned wistful as we were saying goodbye. He seemed to have especially enjoyed the attentions of Amanda and Deb, and he repeatedly invited them to come see him again. As I steered my car onto the blacktop and accelerated, the rear-view mirror framed a picture of him looking forlorn as he stood by the roadside with his hand raised.

For better or worse, James Harold Jennnings' life would never be the same after our visit. I drove back to see him twice within the following week, and I started selectively taking other friends out to meet him and admire his work, which became the subject of rapidly growing interest and media attention.

4. SNOWFLAKES

When literary critic Hugh Kenner called Jargon the "custodian of snowflakes," he was metaphorically commenting on the individuals the press celebrated and the ephemerality of their work. Had it not been for Jargon's preserving it in book form, it would have probably melted away, in effect. In this regard the Southern Visionary Folk Art Preservation Project was consistent with the ongoing mission.

James Harold Jennings—case in point—was such a slight, retiring character that he would have likely been overlooked and forgotten were it not for the attention the Jargon Society brought him.

The difference between what Jargon had always done and what it aimed to do with the Folk Art Project was a matter of material. It was one thing to preserve a body of literary work in print and quite another to preserve unwieldy, built-in works of homemade art and architecture wherever they happened to be, forever subject to the weather and the whims of neighbors, family members, and random passersby. The society had an impressive record in the former case and no experience at all in the latter. The only reason we got away with our audacious project was that no one else was doing it, or almost no one else.

In fact our efforts paralleled those of Seymour Rosen and his Los Angeles organization SPACES—acronymous for Saving and Preserving Art and Cultural EnvironmentS. But Rosen's one-man operation was hardly adequate for its self-defined mission. Out of practical necessity its efforts were limited to the western half of the country, from California to the Midwest. Jonathan and I had been in touch with Rosen, whom we'd met at a folk-art conference the previous year. He welcomed and endorsed our initiative in the South, a region he'd never visited as of 1984.

Also limited was our knowledge of the contemporary folk-art field. I was just beginning to read the existing literature. Meanwhile, our research was conducted on the ground, unsystematically, in personal encounters with the artists in the midst of the private worlds they had created. Many of them were getting on in years, so there was a certain urgency to the effort.

*

In service to the Jargon Society's core mission of publishing and disseminating high-quality books, my job's most mechanical requirement was filling book orders. Jargon publications were shipped to bookstores and libraries from the New Jersey warehouse of Inland Book Company, our distributor, but I supplied copies to private individuals—a chore I'd been accustomed to performing for my own small press in Atlanta, and one that was easily dispatched.

In 1982 Jargon had published *The Last Lunar Baedeker*, a posthumous, 300-page collection of poetry by proto-modernist polymath Mina Loy. I shipped out a few copies of that one every month, and occasionally other books Jargon published in the same year—Tom Meyer's newest, *Sappho's Raft*, and *The Photographs of Lyle Bongé*. There were also sporadic sales of William Anthony's *Bible Stories* and a few others. The early titles that had made Jargon famous in its obscure, underground way were long out of print and sought-after by rare-book collectors.

Nearing publication when I entered the scene was a book of John Menapace's photographs, *Letter in a Klein bottle*—a big, squarish coffee-table book. It came out in the summer of '84, in conjunction with an exhibition at the North Carolina Museum of Art in Raleigh. The opening reception was my first time formally representing the Jargon Society. Jonathan and Tom were away in England.

All I knew about Menapace was the photographs—stark, impeccably composed images of outdoor spaces containing a few architectural elements and no people or other living beings. Innumerable shades of gray. The analogy to minimalist poetry was clear. The photographs had a haunting, austere quality that was amplified when they were grouped.

The photographer himself proved to be as much a character as Saint EOM or Howard Finster—or, for that matter, Jonathan Williams. An adjunct professor of photography at Duke University, Menapace lived in nearby Chapel Hill and was a cult figure among younger photographers and photography enthusiasts in the region. He was about Jonathan's age, late fifties, with long silver hair tied in a ponytail, and terrible posture. His daily uniform consisted of a blue work shirt, faded blue jeans, two-toned sneakers, and, if the weather was cool, a well-seasoned black leather jacket. He was a lively conversationalist—literate and opinionated but sometimes hard to understand, invariably slouched over and muttering into the cigarette that was never far from his lips after it popped out of the pocket-sized tobacco-rolling gizmo he carried with him everywhere.

I liked him instantly, ditto his significant other, Elizabeth Matheson. A serious photographer in her own right, Elizabeth was also beautiful and elegant—a pale-skinned natural blond, always perfectly dressed and coiffed without appearing to have exerted any effort toward the effect. She was from an old North Carolina family and had the accent and manners to prove it. Probably in her forties, but you could tell she would be effortlessly striking and charismatic at any age. They were an interesting couple even at a distance, and much more so up close and in conversation. I was charmed.

Aside from filling book orders, representing the society at official events, and working on the Folk Art Project, I devoted much of my on-duty time to writing grants and fundraising letters, along with a monthly letter to the Jargon Board reporting on recent activities and developments from the home office. It was definitely more than a half-time job.

Toward the end of the year I arranged to have the office's walls painted, covering the patterned wallpaper with white paint that was a more effective background for the plethora of art on display. I hired my college friend Libby Floweree to do the honors. Having started her own house-painting business in Concord, North Carolina, she spent a weekend on the job, assisted by Deb Coffin and me. The temperature dropped precipitously and several inches of snow fell in the late-night hours when we were finishing the job. I returned to my apartment to find the pipes frozen.

5. TREEHOUSE

During my years in Atlanta I had enjoyed following the homegrown music scene in Athens, Georgia, about an hour's drive away. I wrote an article about the B-52's early in their career, and I'd attended many Atlanta shows by the B's and other Athens music ensembles like Pylon, Love Tractor, and the Method Actors. I was aware that members of several bands were former students in the University of Georgia's art department, and that a few of the department's professors were visionary folk-art enthusiasts.

Art Rosenbaum was a neo-expressionist painter, banjo picker, and folk-culture scholar who had documented Howard Finster, among countless others. Judith McWillie, who taught drawing and painting, was quietly conducting groundbreaking research on African American yard art. And Andy Nasisse was a ceramic sculptor who collected works by a range of self-taught visionaries. These professors had shared their enthusiasm for this non-academic art with their students, and some of the students had become devotees.

Michael Stipe, for example, had dropped out of the art school to become the lead singer for R.E.M., fast becoming Athens' most widely known band. The video for their first single, "Radio Free Europe," was filmed in

Finster's Paradise Garden, and Finster collaborated with Stipe to create the cover painting for the band's latest LP, *Reckoning*—a dark image of a corpulent snake emblazoned with handwritten song titles.

Reckoning also had a strong North Carolina connection. It was recorded in Charlotte, and its co-producers Don Dixon and Mitch Easter were linchpin figures in North Carolina's independent-music scene. Mitch was a Winston-Salem native who led the indy pop band Let's Active and had famously transformed the garage at his parents' house into a recording studio.

I was a fan. I owned a copy of Let's Active's LP *Cypress*, likewise R.E.M.'s two albums and their EP *Chronic Town*. I'd seen R.E.M. live on a few occasions, including two great shows that year—one in January in Atlanta, and the other in late September at Duke University, after I'd moved to North Carolina.

Given our apparent mutual interests, I figured I needed to meet Michael Stipe.

My brother Hunter had attended law school at the University of Georgia and was a passing acquaintance, but he no longer lived in Athens. He suggested I contact Michael through their mutual friend Jerry Ayers, to whom he'd introduced me a few years earlier. I had also seen Jerry onstage with Limbo District, one of Athens' most original and unusual bands, unfortunately defunct by late '84.

So I arranged to meet Jerry Ayers in early December, during a solo trip to Georgia in a rented cargo van, to round up work for our exhibition. I planned to be in Athens anyway to see Andy Nasisse and Dilmus Hall.

Hall lived in an African American neighborhood west of downtown Athens, where he had installed several expressive, spiritually referenced painted-concrete sculptures under the big magnolia tree in front of his concrete-block house on Dearing Street. I'd learned about him from the B-52's, and had written about him for *Brown's Guide to Georgia*, the erstwhile travel magazine that employed me for several years.

Hall's most distinctive piece of yard art was a black leather men's shoe displayed under a hand-painted sign, "THE SHOE THAT ROAD THE HOWLING TORNADO." Installed in a wood-framed, glass-panel box supported by metal pipes implanted in the ground, it faced the street in front of his house.

He told me he found the shoe among the rubble in downtown Athens after a tornado in 1973. It still looked brand new.

"That shoe ain't never been on a foot!" Hall declared.

He was struck by the mystery surrounding its origins and the potentially great distance it might have traveled on the fierce winds.

"No telling where that shoe come from!" he mused.

Hall's house was only a mile from Jerry Ayers' one-story Victorian cottage on Meigs Street. After phoning in advance I showed up there around the middle of the day, and Jerry invited me in. I found him drinking tea with a fellow named John Seawright, and he fetched me a cup too.

John was Jerry's housemate, a graceful string-bean dressed in jeans and work boots, a wrinkled white dress shirt, and a well-worn corduroy jacket matching his mop of brown hair. He sat on a couch with one ankle resting on the opposite knee. Physically he reminded me vaguely of myself ten years earlier, although he was definitely taller and longer-legged. There was something of the courtly Old South in his demeanor and his way of speaking.

Jerry was beautiful and birdlike, just as I remembered him—slender, androgynous, and naturally elegant even in his thrift-store clothes. His sensitive, sculpted-looking face registered an active mind, a playful spirit, and a rare inner serenity.

We drank tea and talked, and I told the two of them a little about the Jargon Society and the exhibition we were putting together. Both John and Jerry knew Howard Finster, and Jerry had recently spent a week helping Finster work on his garden.

At Jerry's prodding John read a few of his poems aloud—surreal, southern-gothic dream texts and narrative ballads, fun to hear. After his brief performance Jerry showed me a painting he'd just finished, an enigmatic interaction between two figures wearing black and white stripes under a yellow-hued carnival tent.

At some point during this exchange Jerry suggested we take a walk. It was a warm, Indian-summer day, early afternoon, with remnant storm clouds dappling an otherwise clear, brightly sunlit sky. A couple of blocks from Jerry's house was the Taco Stand, a dining mainstay for budget-conscious university students. In the outdoor seating area alongside the parking lot we encountered a group of student artists and musicians, all of whom looked younger than the three of us. Jerry and John seemed to know them all, and we easily joined their conversation.

One guy with dark curls falling around his two-toned horn-rimmed glasses wore a baggy, brown, thrift-store suit with a wristwatch safety-pinned to the jacket lapel. He walked up to me and said in a subdued, deep voice that he'd been wanting to meet me. He said he'd read some of my magazine articles.

Clasping hands with Michael Stipe, I heard myself nonchalantly reply, "I've been wanting to meet you, too."

Several of us ordered coffee and/or cheap Mexican food, and we sat for a while at a covered picnic table. Michael was just back from a tour of the U.K., where R.E.M. had played to enthusiastic crowds. I mentioned the shows I'd seen earlier in the year, and he was obviously pleased to know I was a fan. After we finished eating and drinking, he walked back over to Jerry's house with us. John Seawright said he would see us later as he split off to walk downtown.

In the crown of a huge, ancient oak tree in Jerry's backyard was a treehouse built from scrap lumber and windows salvaged from the wreckage of torn-down houses. Jerry, Michael, and I climbed the ladder and spent the next half hour sitting in the treehouse talking about art and other subjects of mutual interest.

Jerry was the eldest of our trio—in his late thirties at the time—and had certainly led the most interesting life. He'd grown up in Athens, where his dad was a professor of religion and philosophy at the university. He'd gone to college in the Northeast but dropped out to join the loosely-knit crew at Andy Warhol's New York studio, the Factory. He'd taken on a superstar persona (Silva Thin) and a role as secretary and scribe to the pale one. A few years later he returned to Athens, he said, because he missed the trees and the flowers and the southern springtime. He seemed to know everyone on the Athens scene, and—aside from his great work with Limbo District—he had co-written songs for both the B-52's and R.E.M.

Michael was the youngest, only twenty-four. At my prodding he talked a little about growing up in St. Louis and Atlanta, which he said he hated. On the whole he seemed disinterested in talking about his past, and he turned the questioning to me.

"What's the Jargon Society?" he wanted to know. "Tell me in twenty-five words or less."

"It's a non-profit publishing house that a poet named Jonathan Williams started in 1951 and ran for a few years out of Black Mountain College," I said, then added: "Stop me when I've reached my word limit.""

"Stop!" said Michael, laughing. "Just kidding. Tell me more."

"Jargon's dubious claim to fame is that Jonathan rejected Allen Ginsberg's 'Howl' before Ginsberg sent it on to City Lights. In the 1950s and early '60s Jargon published Henry Miller and Buckminster Fuller and Robert Creeley. And Charles Olson, if you know who he was. Robert Rauschenberg did the cover drawing for an early Jargon chapbook, when he and Jonathan were both students at Black Mountain. And Jargon's going to publish the book I'm working on about Saint EOM."

Jerry and Michael expressed a mutual desire to meet EOM and visit his place. They were also interested in meeting Jonathan. Michael noted that his dad grew up in the town of Black Mountain, North Carolina.

I had already told them about the Finster book, also in the works, and I added that funds to publish the books would come from grants and tax-deductible contributions. I didn't mention it at the time, but I'd gotten it into my head that R.E.M. might play a benefit show for Jargon's Folk Art Project. The last Atlanta show I'd seen by the band was a benefit for an alliance of environmental-defense attorneys.

"I kept a daily journal during the week I spent working with Howard," Jerry said. "I'd be glad to let you see it."

I told him I'd love to read it.

Michael was quiet, seemingly lost in thought. Then he glanced at the wrist watch on his lapel and said he had an appointment.

We climbed down from the treehouse and a few minutes later went our separate ways.

6. INSTALLATION

The weeks spanning the New Year found me occupied with plans for the art exhibition and the annual Jargon board meeting. I drove to Georgia again, combining Christmas at my parents' house with stops in Atlanta and at Pasaquan, Paradise Garden, and Ruben Miller's "Windmill Hill," among other locations. There was still work to be picked up for the exhibition, set to open in less than three weeks.

Time and money were too short to produce a proper catalog, but Jargon was able to fund a twelve-panel foldout brochure illustrated with black-and-white photos of the artists and their work. Roger and I wrote the text, in the form of two brief essays and biographical sketches of the artists, or at least some of them. Roger made most of the photographs, excepting Guy Mendes' striking portrait of a ceremonially garbed Saint EOM on the front cover. I did the rudimentary design and oversaw production by a local printing company. Some of the text was excerpted in a press release I sent out to selected news outlets, in each case accompanied by a couple of photographs.

We filled the storage room at the Sawtooth Center with pieces Roger and I had rounded up for the show. The only missing components were the promised loans from Robert Lynch—about twenty pieces I had identified during a visit to his house. Lynch had assured me he'd personally transport the art to Winston-Salem, but he postponed the trip a couple of times. Only a few days remained before we were to start installing the show, and I was getting nervous.

I was relieved when Robert phoned to let me know he and some friends had just loaded a van with art. They would be on the road in minutes, he assured me. It was already late afternoon, and they had about 175 miles to cover on a route that would take them through rush-hour commuter traffic in Raleigh-Durham.

I figured they wouldn't arrive before eight p.m., so I took a break for dinner and returned to my office sometime after seven. It would be too late to get into the storage room at the Sawtooth Building, but I figured I could keep the Lynch-collection pieces in my office for a few days.

Finally, after midnight, I heard a vehicle pull into the driveway behind our building. I opened the back door to find Robert and two younger men removing large, painted-wood sculptures from the back of a slick-looking, custom-detailed van.

As usual, Robert was turned out as if for a high-powered legal meeting, wearing a camel-hair overcoat, a stylish brown suit, and a jazzy, intricately patterned necktie in complementary colors. He introduced me to his helpers, Ben and Andre, strapping lads who looked like bodyguards. They were practically bundled up against the cold winter weather, and they hardly uttered a word. I joined the three of them to help bring everything inside. By the time we finished, almost every square inch of floor space in my office was filled with art.

Not only had Robert brought the pieces I requested, but he'd also taken the liberty of selecting at least as many others he deemed too good not to include in the show. Among these were a carved, scrap-wood chair by Leroy Person, more of Vernon Burwell's concrete sculptures, and a couple of QJ Stephenson's largest zoomorphic assemblages of driftwood, seashells, fossil rocks, Indian arrowheads, and other materials QJ found in the woods.

Especially prominent among the last-minute additions were two of Jeff Williams' painted figures—life-sized if not larger—each carved from a single tree trunk. One of them was a male nude with chocolate-brown skin, an Afro hair helmet, and heroically scaled genitals. The other was intended as a portrait of Abraham Lincoln.

I offered coffee to my late-night visitors, and I found a box of snack cookies in one of the kitchen cabinets. Since the newly delivered art occupied all the remaining space in my office, we stood in the kitchen and talked for a few minutes. Robert said he wouldn't be able to attend the January twenty-fifth reception, but he planned to return to see the exhibition before that date.

The art transaction was completely informal—no signatures or papers exchanged except for a handwritten list I compiled on the spot. I promised Robert we would take good care of his loan pieces, then he and his helpers climbed into the van and headed back to Halifax County.

We wouldn't be allowed to start installing the show until Monday before the Friday it was set to go on view. With some 200 individual pieces to display and light, we had to work hard and fast.

*

Roger drove over from Durham on Sunday night, and we were joined at the gallery on Monday morning by a few volunteers, including Deb Coffin, her Brit friend Bev Horlick, and SECCA curator Richard Craven, whose alter-ego was the prolific artist-prankster Richard C.

A longtime aficionado of vernacular art, Richard had been working on a similar if more professionally managed show for SECCA, as it turned out, but his "Contemporary Southeastern Folk Art" wouldn't open until the following year. Even though we'd inadvertently stolen his curatorial thunder, he seemed to possess boundless, selfless enthusiasm for our project. He spent hours with us that week, helping us to position and light art of all shapes and sizes.

We'd gathered all this art without reference to the gallery's spatial constraints, and we were determined to show it all. We suspended a number of pieces from the ceiling, and much of the floor space was filled with sculptures on pedestals or simply freestanding on the floor. It was a very oddly designed space, with some areas where average-height adults had to duck in order to navigate under an unusually low ceiling. Not the case in the central part of the gallery, which had no ceiling. Instead, it was open to a large, oval-shaped well in the street-level atrium above. Vertically elongated walls at opposite ends of the oval connected the original factory building's upper-story ceiling to the lower-level gallery floor. All of these elements had been added in the building's clunkily idiosyncratic redesign. In architectural terms the two facing walls were non-load-bearing, although one of them was integrated with a spiral staircase that served as the gallery's main entrance—also added in the redesign.

We used the opposite wall to display scores of the boldly colored masks we'd borrowed from L-15, as Bernard Schatz had decided to start billing himself. We had also borrowed many of his other available pieces. A prolific, culturally sophisticated artist, he was an odd fit with the rustic characters who dominated our selection. He'd come to our attention by way of Jargon board member Ray Kass, a painter and art professor at Virginia Tech in Blacksburg.

An unlikely character in every respect, Schatz was a California transplant to southern Appalachia, a visual artist and performer who'd attended medical school at UCLA and formerly directed a physical-therapy clinic. In the early 1960s as "Cheyanne Schatz, World's Greatest One Man Band," he'd been a fixture on the Los Angeles folk-music scene and made multiple TV appearances on the *Steve Allen Show*.

More recently Schatz had bought the fifty-acre farm where he'd moved with his wife and their young daughter. I had only seen a few of his pieces at Ray's house, but I'd been so taken with them I'd decided he was a must for our show. And besides, Schatz—I mean L-15—was anything but a mainstream artist. He truly belonged in a category all his own.

In the fall of 1984 Roger and Jonathan visited Schatz and beheld for the first time his horde of garishly painted sculptures and other works stored in a windowless, tarpaper-covered outbuilding on his secluded property. Roger brought back a van-load of his work on loan, and we were keen to display all of it in our show, including dozens of velvet-eyed masks, an array of cartoonish "Inquisition Torture Instruments," and several boxes of intricately painted "Hex Blocks"—bits of scrap wood, each painted with a wide-eyed face and pierced with a single nail, like a pin in a Voodoo doll.

While we were installing the show I made multiple trips back and forth to the Jargon office, where I fielded calls from reporters who'd seen my press release. A couple of them met us at the gallery, where we showed them some of the work and talked with them about the artists. Press photographers arrived later.

The first article appeared in the *Winston-Salem Sentinel* on Thursday afternoon, while we were still rushing to finish the installation. A profusely illustrated, full-page feature article followed in Friday morning's *Winston-Salem Journal.* Curious members of the public started arriving before noon. We were still busy making adjustments and posting wall labels.

One early visitor was Ruth Julian, a longtime community arts leader who, with her attorney husband Ira, had built one of Winston-Salem's largest contemporary-art collections. She was in her seventies and supremely confident in her views about art. I could tell she was still trying to decide what she thought about this visionary folk art. She called my attention to one of L-15's sculptures and asked if it was for sale, and if so, for how much.

Most of the exhibited work was not for sale, but L-15 had priced all of his pieces. Consulting his list, I quoted the price to her—something like $450.

Her jaw dropped, and she said, "Who does he think he is? Picasso?"

"Oh, he's better than Picasso," I retorted.

Obviously missing my playful intent, she fixed me

with a baleful stare, her eyes hurling daggers.

Later that morning I spied another distinguished visitor, namely local indy-rock producer and musician Mitch Easter. With his baby face, unruly shock of two-toned hair, and casual hipster attire he was instantly recognizable from photos I'd seen. He and four other young, hip-looking guys wearing dark clothes were admiring and discussing Howard Finster's *Duck Woman of Orpliss*. I stopped what I was doing and walked over to say hello and introduce myself. I told Mitch I was a fan, and he introduced me to his companions, who constituted the British punk band Echo and the Bunnymen. They were taking a break from a recording session at the Drive-In Studio, as Mitch had named the famously converted garage.

"I saw the article in today's paper," Mitch said, "then I remembered Michael Stipe telling me this show would be happening soon. So we decided to come over and see it." Gesturing toward the *Duck Woman* he added, "I love Howard Finster's work."

7. MORE THAN YOU CAN SHAKE A STICK AT

There was no standard profile or template for the artists who interested us. In our shared conception "visionary folk art" was a broad, open-ended category. The artists came from varied cultural backgrounds and many walks of life.

Leroy Almon was an African American cop in the small-town South. Before becoming a police dispatcher in Tallapoosa, Georgia, he was a salesman for the Coca-Cola Company. Introduced to his painted relief carvings a couple of years earlier at Judith Alexander's gallery in Atlanta, I had driven to see him in Tallapoosa soon afterward.

In a prior stage of his adult life Almon lived in Columbus, Ohio, where he apprenticed with the widely known woodcarving barber Elijah Pierce. He had developed a style of carving and painting derived from Pierce's and was taking it in his own direction. Relatively young, still in his forties, Almon was a middle-class guy living with his family in a suburban ranch house. To supplement the modest income from his salaried job he made art.

Almon handed out business cards identifying himself as a folk artist. Like his mentor Pierce, he gravitated toward biblical themes of stark moral contrast—Heaven and Hell, salvation and sin, Jesus and Satan. Shrewdly enterprising, he custom-made a piece that he presented to me when Roger and I arrived to pick up some of his work for our exhibition.

A winged, white-robed angel in this vertical relief carving looked out from a face probably intended as a self-portrait—a handsome, beatifically smiling, brown-skinned man. He carried a golden sphere labeled "FOLK ART"and seemed to be following a sign in the lower left corner that read "WINSTON-SALEM CITY LIMITS." Nearby he had incised "THE PATTERSONS" in smaller, less prominent letters.

Several of Almon's larger, more ambitious pieces were on hand, but he had set them aside for specific collectors or potential direct sales, and was reluctant to lend any of them for our exhibition. We had to settle for the angel piece—for which I paid Almon fifty dollars, his asking price—and a few other small relief carvings, including one that featured a horned devil's head on a snake's sleek, fiery red body.

Back in Winston-Salem we installed Almon's folk-art angel on a narrow, freestanding wall at the top of the spiral staircase, where it functioned as a kind of invitation to the exhibit below.

Not that one was needed. The well in the ground-floor

atrium revealed enough to spark the curiosity of sentient passersby. More than a few were spontaneously drawn downstairs to join others who'd planned their visits in advance.

Central to my early ideas for the exhibition, of course, were Saint EOM and Howard Finster. Their masterpieces were the multi-acre environments they'd created in their rural yards—Pasaquan and Paradise Garden—visionary siteworks built into the ground. Fortunately, both artists also made freestanding pieces, and a few of their larger ones helped anchor the sprawling selection.

EOM's boldly painted, life-size concrete bust of a smiling, brown-skinned man wearing an elaborate, beaded headdress was shown alongside a painting he'd made on a three-foot sheet of plywood—a composite image of abstracted, tattooed arms and legs entwined in yogic postures. Finster's *Duck Woman of Orpliss*—a ridiculous-looking, pink-skinned, duckbilled humanoid, rendered in brightly painted cutout plywood—was paired with his life-size cutout bust of a blue-robed, winged angel prayerfully posed in profile.

Likewise noticeable from some distance were Jeff Williams' two painted figures carved from tree trunks, among the pieces loaned by Robert Lynch. The youngest artist represented in the show, Williams was in his late twenties, and he earned a living as a carpenter and automobile mechanic. Also loaned by Robert Lynch were most of the exhibited works by Leroy Person, a retired, African American sawmill worker from the eastern North Carolina township of Occoneechee Neck.

Person's two extensively carved, slapdash wooden chairs were also linchpin components. One was painted a somber brown, while the other featured bold shades of blue, yellow, and red. The chairs drew attention to Person's wonderful, smaller pieces— decoratively incised, abstracted birds and animals that had a monumental quality even though they weren't much larger than standard chess pieces. He had identified a number of these smaller pieces as "peafowl," although the resemblance was elusive. Some were colored with melted crayon wax.

Person was in his seventies by the time Roger Manley and Robert Lynch met him. I missed out. Sadly, he died of respiratory failure within days of our show's opening.

Herman Bridgers was an African American preacher in the same part of North Carolina, independently encountered earlier by both Roger and Robert. It was his sentinel cutouts that caught their attention—black-outlined white figures with stiffly outstretched arms— posted in front of his whitewashed concrete-block church alongside Highway 301 north of Rocky Mount. Striking from a distance despite their modest size, these figures represented "church mens," in Bridgers' phrase, which I interpreted to mean members of his church, posed as if they were flagging down drivers. We included a couple of Bridgers' similar figures in the show.

Dilmus Hall's two compact, sculptural tableaux stood for his two favored subjects—secular and sacred life. In one, a blobby little clay figure emerged from an outhouse with the word "TIOLET" painted on the door—a one-word poem, as Jonathan observed. Hall's other tableau was a reductive Crucifixion scene, in which the faces of Jesus and his two criminal companions were impaled by wooden toothpicks. Both pieces were painted in high-contrast red and black, the official colors of the University of Georgia Bulldogs football team. The figures' bulging, startled-looking eyes were faux-pearl beads.

Also in the show were a few of Hall's ball-point-pen drawings, whose gesticulating figures looked related to Bridgers' church mens.

Sam Doyle's paintings on roofing-tin slabs typically portrayed his neighbors and historical figures associated with Frogmore, his community on St. Helena Island, South Carolina. Our exhibition included a pair of paintings that Jonathan had bought from Doyle—portraits of two root doctors, traditional healers known as Doctor Buzzard (DR BUZ) and Doctor Crow (DR CROW), normally on display in the Jargon office.

A bleached conch shell was attached to one of DR BUZ's ears, illustrating a seashell "telephone" by which he reportedly communicated with the spirit world. "HALO," he was saying, answering the spiritual call.

Raymond Coins' Nativity scene of carved-stone figures was starkly impressive, as was Annie Hooper's embellished-driftwood reenactment of King Belshazar's Feast, a more expressionistic take on a scene from the Old Testament book of Daniel, with its apparition of mysterious, golden writing on the wall.

L-15's work stood out by virtue of its profusion, extravagance of bold color, and figural idiosyncrasies.

A highlight that normally graced Roger's living room was William Owens' boldly painted, carved-wood tableau of a white-bearded Uncle Sam figure alongside a pretty, dark-skinned angel, joined in holding forth a big slice of watermelon symbolically offered to the viewer. *Separation of Church and State*, Owens had titled it.

More roughly hewn were Clyde Jones' "critters" assembled from scrap timber and other materials he found near his home overlooking the Haw River south of Chapel Hill. Several of them were scattered about the gallery floor in our exhibition, like free-ranging wild pigs.

The clay sculptures and figurally embellished vessels by Georgia Blizzard of Glade Spring, Virginia, were smaller and more unobtrusive but extremely powerful when viewed up close, revealing visionary details worthy of William Blake.

James Harold Jennings' work was prominently featured, as I'd promised him. Although vocally skeptical about conventional religion—"Them Christian preachers, all they want is you money," he once told me—Jennings incorporated images of white-robed angels into a number of the pieces he made during that phase of his career. They would have dominated our selection of his painted wood assemblages and wind-powered gizmos had it not been for his big Ferris wheel, the largest piece he'd made to date—promptly purchased from the exhibition by Jargon board member Ray Kass.

Eventually I talked Jennings into seeing the show. His brother Clyde drove him to Winston-Salem on a weekday morning to have a look when few other viewers were in the gallery. From what I could tell, he wasn't especially impressed.

8. GUEST LIST

I was glad I'd allowed a two-week lag between the exhibition's opening date and the formal reception, set to coincide with the Jargon board-meeting weekend starting on January twenty-fifth. In the meantime I was busily sorting out details pertaining to the meeting and related festivities. Not least among these was the guest list for a Friday-evening cocktail party at Philip Hanes' house and a special dinner he was to host after the events at the Sawtooth Center. Since I was keeping track of everyone expected at the board meeting, including several special guests, Philip charged me with compiling the list.

"Let's try to keep it to thirty people," he suggested during a phone conversation.

I reviewed my notes and dutifully included everyone's name on the invitation list for the Friday dinner and after-party, along with spouses or partners when applicable. I counted thirty-five names on the list. Close enough, I figured.

"I said let's keep it to *thirty people!*" Philip thundered when he phoned me after receiving the list. "There are thirty-*five* names on this list!"

Taken aback, I replied, "Yes. That's just the way it worked out."

"When I said keep it to thirty people, I meant *keep it to thirty people!*" Philip barked.

I collected my thoughts. "Ahhh....All right, no problem," I finally said. "I'll revise the list and make sure the invitations only go out to thirty people."

"I don't even know who some of these people are!" Philip continued. "Who is Hunter Patterson. Is he some relation to you?"

"Hunter is my brother. He's driving up from Atlanta, and I was going to bring him as my guest."

"Well, he's got nothing to do with the board meeting, and I don't see any reason for him to be at my house on Friday night."

"I've put Hunter in charge of entertaining Robert Bishop, whose name you'll see on the list. The director of the Museum of American Folk Art in New York. He'll be here all weekend, and he'll need someone to pay attention to him and drive him around when he's not giving his talk, which is the reason we're bringing him here. I'll be too busy, so Hunter agreed to do that. I was going to introduce them at the cocktail party."

"Yes, of course I know who Robert Bishop is, and I certainly want him there. But anyway, as I said, I want the invitations limited to thirty people."

I didn't wait for Philip to question other names on the list. I just told him to consider it done, then I hung up.

Instead of walking upstairs I phoned Whitney and told him about the conversation I'd just had with Philip. "If

Hunter's not invited, I'm not going," I told him.

"I don't blame you," he said. "I won't go either."

The cocktail party was to be at Philip's eighteenth-century plantation house, which had been dismantled on its original site in rural North Carolina, then painstakingly reconstructed and restored on the wooded Hanes estate in suburban northwest Winston. The dinner party was booked at Zevely House, a pricey but consistent restaurant in a Colonial-era brick home near the Jargon office.

Philip's wife Joan had been dead for a year. She seemed to have been universally adored, although I never had the pleasure of meeting her. Fifty-eight-year-old Philip had recently started romancing his physical therapist Charlotte Metz, whose rural background set her well apart from everyone involved in the Jargon Society. Although she hadn't manifested any interest in literary arcana or visionary art, she would be Philip's companion for the Jargon weekend's social events. They would be married within the year.

Further ensuring a lively time for all during that weekend, a crew from the MTV show *The Cutting Edge* contacted me a few days after we installed the exhibition. They would be in North Carolina during the last week in January to film a special on North Carolina' independent music scene. The half-hour weekly program was produced by IRS Records, R.E.M.'s label. The director wanted to film not only some of the region's young bands and musical performers, but also other examples of regional culture. The "Southern Visionary Folk Artists" exhibition had been recommended, and I'd agreed to let the crew film in the gallery for most of the day on Friday.

Set to arrive that same day along with the MTV crew, various Jargon board members, and other special guests, was featured artist Bernard Schatz, aka L-15, who had promised to give a "lecture" after the evening's festivities in the gallery. He showed up about an hour ahead of the folks from *The Cutting Edge*.

"L-15," he introduced himself, offering his hand. "But you can just call me 'L.'"

Accompanying him outside to the rented station wagon he'd driven from Virginia, I helped him bring in several boxes of what he said were props and costumes for his lecture. When the MTV crew arrived, he promptly monopolized their attention, and he kept them busy for the better part of an hour, surrounded by his work and discoursing about selected pieces.

Wearing a long, black cape—and at times a matching hood that concealed his entire head and face—L-15 brandished a multicolored, wand-like object from his "Inquisition Torture Instruments" series, pointing it at individual sculptures that he talked about like a carnival huckster. He seemed to take special delight in showing off dozens of pieces that looked rather like partially melted miniature bar-bells, white on either end with an abstract-expressionist mix of bold colors on their connecting stems. Each one represented the aorta of a famous historical figure, he explained before he began holding them up one at a time and reciting their titles: *Aorta of William Shakespeare, Aorta of Sigmund Freud, Aorta of Abraham Lincoln, Aorta of Adolf Hitler,* etc. It didn't take long to figure out that the smallest aortas were identified with the most reviled individuals. Hitler's wasn't much bigger than an earthworm.

Meanwhile, out-of-town board members and invited guests were arriving at various times during the day. I had made arrangements for those flying into the Greensboro airport to be ferried to hotels where rooms had been reserved for them. Awaiting them were weekend schedules indicating times and locations for all pre-planned events.

Hunter drove into town around mid-afternoon, as expected, just in time for me to give him a brief tour of the exhibition and get us back to my apartment so I could change clothes.

9. THREE-RING CIRCUS

The reception started at six p.m., and by six-thirty the gallery was jammed with people—at least 300 in addition to Jargon board members and others in the official party. About twenty-five of them came directly from the elite gathering at Philip's home.

The Cutting Edge crew was filming it all.

At one point when attendance was at its peak, I was in the atrium, about to descend the spiral staircase to the gallery, when SECCA Director Ted Potter sidled up to me and complimented me on the turnout.

"How did you do this?!" he marveled. "We're always trying to get crowds like this for openings at SECCA."

"We got very good press—that's all I know." I had to raise my voice to be heard over the buzz of conversation. We moved away from the stairs and leaned forward with our elbows on the waist-high wall around the well to the floor below, where we observed the mingling, gawking people.

"I noticed! But how did you make that happen? We have a full-time p.r. person on our staff, and we never get the kind of press coverage you got for this show."

"Novelty," I said. "The Jargon Society's new in town. Or at least our office is new. My press releases and Roger's photographs must have gotten people's attention."

"Well, it's just amazing," Ted observed as we watched the crowd in the gallery.

While Ted and I talked, inner-circle representatives of the Cosmic Ray Deflection Society of North America were arriving out front. At the request of Chuck Alston/ Also Aswell I had borrowed a couple of orange traffic cones from the local police department and placed them at the edge of the street directly in front of the Sawtooth entrance to reserve a special parking spot for the Cosmic Raymobile. The heavy-glass doors at the entrance swung wide to accommodate Also and his entourage.

Even though they were attired in their tin-foil hats and individually decorated costumes, almost no one batted an eye when they descended the stairs into the crowded gallery. The Cosmic Ray crew was no competition for the art. Like everyone else, they promptly immersed themselves in looking at the exhibition, studying the wall labels, and sampling the free wine and hors d'oeuvres being doled out from a long table at one end of the gallery.

Meanwhile, upstairs in the auditorium, a standing-room-only crowd awaited the promised lectures.

Those proceedings began shortly after seven p.m. with my brief opening remarks and introduction of the featured speaker, Robert Bishop, executive director of New York's Museum of American Folk Art.

Jonathan, Tom Meyer, and I had met Bishop in Georgia

at a surprise birthday party for Howard Finster in 1983. In subsequent correspondence Bishop had encouraged our pursuit of the Folk Art Project, and I'd kept him posted about related developments. After I moved to Winston-Salem to open the Jargon office, he accepted my invitation to give a brief talk at the premiere of our show.

Of course he used the occasion to pitch his museum and recruit new supporters, but he also made a broader case for contemporary folk art, and he gave us a ringing endorsement. Commenting on the art downstairs, Bishop told the audience, "The impact of this exhibition will be felt for years to come."

Next on the bill: L-15.

Had I seen the twenty-year-old tapes of Cheyanne Schatz on the Steve Allen Show I might have thought better of it, but at the time I was completely taken with Schatz's prankster schtick and thought, "Why not?" So, after Robert Bishop's talk I introduced him without providing any background information:

"Ladies and gentlemen, L-15."

Whereupon he made his entrance and announced his topic: "My Life as a Southern Visionary Folk Artist."

As he spoke he fumbled to set up an easel on which he placed a sheet of white posterboard bearing the hand-lettered lecture title. He used a wooden baton as a pointer.

Lean and haggard-looking but calm and soothing in

his delivery, Schatz was in his early fifties, and he brought to mind a slightly mad version of Jimmy Stewart. His plaid flannel work shirt was sloppily tucked into his faded blue jeans with part of the shirttail hanging out.

"Now, if you'll just bear with me for a moment, I'm almost ready to begin," he explained as he moved about the stage assembling and adjusting props and repositioning samples of his work. He brought out a portable electric fan at the end of a long extension cord, and he set it up near center stage, pointing it toward a black banner bearing the sewn-on logo "L-15," in white, cutout-felt letters He turned the switch and stood back to inspect the arrangement.

"There!" he said. "I want it to look like it's gently fluttering in the breeze."

Turning to the audience, he said, "That's good, don't you think?"

Next he produced a roll of paper from among the clutter, and he inserted one end of it into a beat-up antique typewriter with a pair of pliers affixed to the carriage, precariously set up on a wooden table he'd dragged out with him. The paper roll contained his lecture notes. Using the pliers to turn the carriage and crank the paper noisily through the typewriter, he began stiffly reading a narrative about the fifty-acre property where he lived in the Southern Appalachian Mountains, and how he'd bought it sight unseen from a real-estate catalog.

As the roll of paper unspooled from the top of the typewriter and into a chaotic pile on the floor, L-15 told about moving his wife and young daughter across the country from Los Angeles to live in a remote site where he could concentrate on his work. He described some of the creative projects he'd taken on since he moved there. He also showed off a few artifacts of his rustic life on the secluded farm, including a pair of battered work boots.

"Boots of southern visionary folk artist," he solemnly announced, holding them up for all to see.

Leaving the "typewriter of visionary folk artist," he continued talking, more off-the-cuff. Speaking excitedly about his new "Eyeballs" series, he noted that several small prototypes were included in the exhibition downstairs, but he explained that that his ultimate plan with the series was far more ambitious. He placed a poster-board drawing on an easel to illustrate the *Giant Eyeball Tower* he planned to erect on his property. The eyeball at the top of the steel-rebar tower would be so large as to be clearly visible to drivers on a nearby interstate-highway curve at the bottom of a mountain less than one mile from his property, as if it were staring at them.

He pointed the baton at a drawing on the easel—a stick-figure poking his head out the window of the crudely drawn car, presumably stopped alongside the highway, with a dash-broken line of sight between the figure's bugged-out eyes and the giant eyeball looming above him.

Tough act to follow.

Fortunately Roger Manley had a dazzling selection of slides to show and clever stories to tell about them—a running commentary on art he'd encountered in out-of-the-way places during his travels across North Carolina. His presentation began with "Jolly" Joshua Samuels' "Can City," alongside a remote rural road in eastern North Carolina—an environment made entirely of emptied steel and aluminum cans attached to a fence around an overgrown field and affixed to wires stretched across the property from trees on either side.

Roger's description of the project as an audience-participation artwork drew a lot of laughs. Local passersby were apparently happy to toss used beer or soft-drink cans out their car windows into the field, he explained. Thus did Jolly Joshua Samuels' garden perpetually grow!

Roger went on to show images of more elaborate, carefully crafted works by artists for whom the term "visionary" was more applicable. His slides of Annie Hooper and her houseful of biblical narrative sculptures made for striking evidence of the dramatic context for her tableaus.

The audience seemed to eagerly follow Roger's talk, receptive to each new artist he introduced. His pacing was good, although I could tell he was rushing in order to cover all the ground he'd staked out. When he switched to his second slide tray after about half an hour at the podium, his talk was jarringly interrupted by Philip Hanes.

"How much longer is this going to go on?" Philip demanded to know. It was a rhetorical question, as it was clear he'd had enough. Still seated, about midway back in the crowded room, he spoke loudly enough to be heard by everyone present.

"Some of us have dinner reservations, and we're already late," he groused.

Roger fielded the awkward moment by excusing Philip and his party—and anyone else who wanted or needed to leave.

"I've got another tray of slides to show anyone who'd like to stay," he offered.

Philip wasn't satisfied. "I think that's enough," he insisted. "We've all been in here for almost two hours. I'm sure everybody needs to go have dinner!"

By that point the audience was already breaking up, and people were filing out the doors. I exchanged stunned looks with Roger, openmouthed and shaking my head in disbelief.

While Philip and his invited guests made their way to Zevely House, I joined Roger, Hunter, L-15, Whitney, Deb, and several others for sandwiches, pizza, salads, and beer at the Rose and Thistle, a popular, informal restaurant tucked against the south side of Interstate 40's infamous Hawthorne Curve. Afterwards we all went back to my place, where we were soon met by Jonathan, Tom Meyer, and others who'd dined with Philip and attended his cocktail party. The after-after-party at my apartment was much livelier, I was assured.

"Some of the guests at Philip's house wondered where Jargon's president and new executive director were," Jonathan drily noted as he lit a fresh cigar.

10. BOARD MEETING

Several of us were bleary-eyed the next morning at the Jargon board meeting, in the banquet room at the Sawtooth Building. A catered breakfast was spread out on a couple of long tables covered with maroon tablecloths. I helped myself to fresh fruit, a croissant, scrambled eggs, and coffee. Several additional fold-up tables had been arranged in an angular U-shape in the middle of the large room, with plastic-seat chairs uniformly arrayed around the outside. Place cards for Jargon's officers faced the chairs lined up at the closed end of the U, and I set my plate and coffee down at my designated spot near the center.

Famished, I dug in. I had nearly polished off my eggs when I spotted Philip Hanes entering through a door at the opposite end of the room. He appeared to be in a good mood, smiling and shaking hands. Then we made eye contact, and he beelined to where I sat sipping coffee.

"I was sorry not to see you at my house last night," he said, sounding cordial and almost contrite as he shook my hand. "You know I never intended to keep you away."

"Wish I hadn't had to miss it," I told him, "but I needed to entertain my brother and L-15 and some of the other people I invited. I didn't want to crowd you. Anyway, I think everybody had a good time. I hope you did."

"Yes indeed," he said, patting my shoulder. "Well, very good. I just wanted to be sure there was no misunderstanding."

"Not at all!"

I smiled as Philip greeted other board members on his way to the buffet table. Surprised and relieved, I got up to fetch more coffee and say good morning to Lucinda Bunnen, the Atlanta photographer and arts patron. I had introduced her to Jonathan a couple of years earlier, and had recently suggested her for membership on Jargon's board, which she would officially join in a few hours. It was good to see a familiar face from Atlanta.

All business board meetings, I presume, focus on what an organization has accomplished and what it aims to do in the near future—and, of course the related expenses and income. So it was with the Jargon board meeting I had attended as a guest in '84, and likewise with this meeting in January 1985.

Thorns Craven delivered a treasurer's report, and minutes from the 1984 meeting were approved. I gave an abbreviated update on the Folk Art Project, of which there was ample evidence in the exhibition downstairs. There followed an extended discussion that reminded me of my curious status in this organization—a newcomer, a lowly research associate, and a sort of figurehead—an executive in name only.

The tenor of the exchange was different from the '84 meeting—more pessimistic for sure. Whitney and Thorns were clearly tired of struggling on behalf of an organization that could barely meet its meager expenses, much less pay them a dime for their services. The more "active" board members—those who contributed the most money, i.e. Philip Hanes and Don Anderson, an oil-company executive from New Mexico—talked as if they were just about tapped out when it came to largesse on Jargon's behalf.

Don, then in his sixties, was the board's senior member. With his striking, sharp-nosed profile, inscrutably intelligent face, and mane of white hair combed straight back, he wore a brown tweed jacket and khakis, but his shoes looked sturdy enough for mountain hiking. The CEO of an oil company in Roswell, New Mexico, Don had no known connection to the UFO mysteries associated with that town. I knew little of his professional life, but it was clear he was a dedicated esthete—a prodigious collector of art, a generous arts patron, and a painter himself.

The consensus at the morning session seemed to be that if Jargon couldn't find new sources of income, then perhaps it should shut down.

Robert Bishop sat in on the meeting's first couple of hours. The discussion probably reminded him of his struggling museum's board. The Museum of American Folk Art was less than twenty-five years old—ten years younger than Jargon—and Bishop had been its director since 1977. Despite long odds, he had successfully pushed for a major expansion of the museum and its mission.

At around noon my brother arrived to rescue Bishop. The orientation I'd given Hunter was evidently sufficient, as he whisked the museum director off to have lunch, then visit Old Salem, Reynolda House, and SECCA—all equally new to both of them. Meanwhile Deb Coffin had assured me she and her children would entertain our other special guest, L-15.

Jargon's founder and publisher had kept mostly quiet during the morning session, which he endured while looking bored and impatient. As board and staff members reconvened in the early afternoon, he put a brown cardboard box on the table. Brandishing the customary cigar, he announced the manuscript of a book that he said could be Jargon's salvation—a cookbook, of all things. It was titled *White Trash Cooking,* and the author was a Florida caterer and part-time photographer named Ernest Matthew Mickler, pronounced *Mike-ler.*

JW gave a brief summary of the box's contents— recipes Mickler had collected from presumably gen-u-ine white-trash friends and acquaintances throughout his native South, along with straightforward color photos made during his travels around the region, in a sort of Walker-Evans-meets-William-Eggleston vein. Then he sent the box circulating around the table so everyone could have a look.

Jonathan had spent much of his adult life "rattling the old Jargon begging bowl," seeking out those rare individuals with the financial wherewithal, idiosyncratic tastes, and singular wisdom to support his publishing endeavors. It had always been a struggle, he reminded the board. Keenly aware of the society's financial troubles, he proposed borrowing the money to publish Mickler's book. The lenders would be a few unnamed "friends of Jargon," whom he was sure could be repaid in a timely manner.

Had he not been a superb pitchman, JW could never have kept an outfit like the Jargon Society going for so many years. His hilarious, cleverly designed form letters soliciting support for various Jargon projects were legendary. Likewise effective was his appeal to the board members that afternoon. He laid it on thick, transmitting his enthusiasm for Mickler's book to others in the room. By the time the meeting was over, Philip and Don had been inspired to lend most of the production costs for 5,000 copies, and new board member Lucinda Bunnen kicked in the rest.

Veterans of Jargon's inner circle had heard these kinds of spiels from Jonathan before, most recently in connection with William Anthony's *Bible Stories*, an abbreviated, fractured summary of the Old Testament, illustrated with Anthony's deliberately awkward drawings. Six years later Jargon was paying to store several thousand unsold copies in boxes of 100 each at the Inland Book Company warehouse in New Jersey

Surely the backers of Ernie's book harbored some doubts as to whether they would ever be repaid.

As for me, I was halfway into my first year of the three-year term I'd been hired to serve, but the day's proceedings reminded me to take nothing for granted. I silently vowed to redouble my fundraising efforts for the Folk Art Project. I figured I needed to raise enough money to cover my salary and as many related expenses as possible. The books on Saint EOM, Howard Finster, et al would surely cost tens of thousands of dollars to produce.

I had my work cut out.

As these thoughts spun through my head I suddenly realized I'd been approved for a $5,000 salary increase. Once again, no one was as surprised as I. Now I had three-quarters of a full-time dream job, but of course it didn't make any real difference in the bigger picture.

Meeting adjourned.

11. PILGRIMAGE

The "Southern Visionary Folk Artists" exhibition continued to draw attention in its final weeks and beyond. Additional coverage in the local and regional media helped bring in a stream of visitors almost every day for as long as it was up. The most thoughtful review appeared a few months later in *Art Papers*.

"We must address the power of these objects to excite a personal experience for the viewer which is direct, without intervening considerations," wrote critic Edward Waddell. "The air of crudity or naïveté is only superficial, for as objects of art they transcend form, penetrating to something more fundamental."

Waddell's prescient conclusion: "The Jargon Society's goal to preserve, document, and exhibit this art will facilitate an accessibility and popular acceptance which may well be the only real safeguard of its integrity."

News of the show spread well beyond the immediate region, and several curious viewers went out of their way to see it. Noteworthy among the latter was Sam Farber, a serious collector from New York, where he was the founder and CEO of Copco, the kitchenware company. Having been tipped off by his friend Robert Bishop, Farber phoned me while making travel arrangements, and we agreed to meet. He flew into the Greensboro airport on a weekday morning and arrived in Winston-Salem early enough to take me out for lunch in exchange for a guided tour of the exhibition.

Sharp of both wit and eye, Farber was in his fifties, fit and compact. Clearly well-versed in the folk- and outsider-art field, he was already familiar with some of the artists in our show, including Finster and Sam Doyle. Others were new to him, though, and he knew nothing about the Jargon Society, so we had plenty to discuss. He talked enthusiastically about the French artist Pascal Verbena, previously unknown to me, and he showed me some photos of the work, which I agreed was very compelling.

From the exhibition Sam bought several pieces, including one of L-15's startling, brightly painted masks, whose round, concave eyes and mouths were lined with black velvet.

During the first weekend in February I hosted a small contingent of folk-art enthusiasts who traveled 275 miles from Athens, Georgia, in a Volkswagen Beetle, ostensibly just to see the exhibition. Two of them— Jerry Ayers and Michael Stipe—I already knew, although I'm not sure I would have recognized Michael with his new look. He'd cut his hair super-short and dyed it dark red.

It was my first time meeting the third member of their party, a quiet, striking woman named Cynthia Williams. Cynthia had long, dark-blond hair, a high forehead, killer cheekbones, and eyes that registered shyness overpowered by an omnivorous curiosity—a trait that surely served her well in her role as a photographer. Somewhere along the way I had acquired a poster advertising R.E.M.'s *Reckoning* LP, which featured her photograph of the *Serpent Mound* in Finster's Paradise Garden.

Jerry and Michael were recently returned from three weeks with artist/collector/university professor Andy Nasisse in southern Mexico—a part of the world I knew well enough to discuss it with them. Jerry wore brightly striped, handwoven pants he'd bought at a street market in Chiapas, along with a misshapen felt hobo hat and a khaki safari jacket covered with original ink-marker art by Howard Finster. Cynthia hadn't been on the Mexico trip, but she wore a dark, pin-striped shawl that Jerry or Michael had brought her as a souvenir.

Michael, wearing a corduroy jean jacket, was subdued and preoccupied, with occasional eruptions of what seemed like obsessive-compulsive behavior. While I drove us around in my car he rode shotgun, occasionally making a comment while busily shredding the thighs of his blue jeans with a razor blade.

They crashed on the floor of my apartment. On their first morning in town Michael got up before the rest of us and shaved a bald spot into the back of his head, *à la* Friar Tuck. I didn't know him well enough to assess his situation, but he seemed uncomfortable in his own skin. At the time I thought he might have been struggling internally with the new reality of being a pop star.

Far was it from me to fault anyone for eccentric behavior. In any case I was honored to host this trio of out-of-town artists. On their first full day in town I took them through the exhibition. Lunch was at the Rainbow, the bookstore and cafe near the Jargon office, where a handful of patrons and staffers obviously recognized Michael but were hip enough not to bug him. Then I led a two-car caravan out to visit James Harold Jennings. Joining my out-of-town guests for the trip were Deb Coffin, Jargon president Whitney Jones, our office neighbor Suzanne Bernardo, and Whitney's teenage son Lindsay, an R.E.M. fan who was clearly awed to be in Michael's presence.

By that time I'd been to see Jennings many times and introduced him to collectors, fellow artists, and curious friends, who were invariably charmed by him. Likewise Jerry, Michael, and Cynthia. They had been taken with the examples of Jennings' work in the exhibition, but they seemed particularly moved by the experience of meeting him and seeing his work on-site.

Michael zeroed in on a small piece Jennings had recently finished—a painted-wood "hornet" with outspread wings and a body cut from a spirally twisted vine. He bought it as soon as Jennings priced it. Twenty-five dollars—at least twice what he would have charged a few months earlier.

During a stop at the Jargon office later that afternoon Michael told me he was unaccustomed to having money, but he liked using it to buy art. He still lived in the rented shotgun shack where I'd visited him, on Barber Street in Athens, and he seemed astonished that his personal income for the previous year had been in the range of $20,000. He shook his head in disbelief.

"I'm sure you earned every penny of it," I said.

*

The half-hour program about North Carolina's music scene aired on February twenty-fourth on MTV's *The Cutting Edge*. Very little of the footage from our exhibition made the cut, although there was a snippet in which Jonathan Williams read a few poems. Barely hinted at was the creative cross-fertilization between visionary folk artists and southern indy-rock bands including R.E.M. and Let's Active, whose music was featured on the program.

12. MUSEUM OF HORROR

Mitch Easter met me at the Jargon office one afternoon with Angie Carlson, a Minneapolis music writer who would soon join his band. I had promised to introduce them to James Harold Jennings, so we got into my car and headed north. Like everyone else I'd taken to meet him, they loved Jennings and his roadside display, and they bought a few things from him.

From Jennings' place I drove us to visit another artist I'd met since I moved to Winston-Salem—Hermon Finney, who operated a concrete lawn-ornament business about an hour to the west, near the Yadkin River.

Finney's studio and workshop overlooked a mostly residential stretch of the main highway through Arlington, North Carolina. Following a tip from Roger Manley, I had first visited the place when I was still new to the region. The business Finney operated with his two rarely seen brothers was marked by two full-size, silver-painted concrete knights in armor, posed with long-handled battle-axes. Guarding the gate to the family compound, these imposing figures could hardly be missed by passing highway traffic. The knights—and the pair of dog-sized sphinxes alongside them—were Finney's own designs, cast and painted in the tin-roofed, open-air workshop where he manufactured generic lawn statuary and created his own distinctive, one-of-a-kind sculptures.

Adjoining the workshop area was a single-story, concrete-block building painted white. A blue-lettered sign over the doorway—"WELCOME TO FANTASTIC ART"—was flanked by matching, life-size relief sculptures of a woman's severed head with blood dripping from her mouth. The little building housed a collection of hand-crafted dioramas Finney had made in the 1950s and '60s, each reflecting a macabre sense of humor and an affinity for the grotesque.

Jake the Red-headed Human Butcher stood at a chopping block dismembering a corpse with a meat cleaver, while his presumed next victim—helplessly shackled in a nearby corner—looked on in horror. Carved and assembled from bits of wood, this ghastly narrative was meticulously painted, as were several other similarly startling scenes encased in handmade, glass-front boxes.

Devils tormented lost souls in the flames of Hell in one diorama. In another, a voluptuous woman wearing a baby-doll nightgown was manacled to the ceiling of a torture chamber where a male victim was stretched out and shackled on a rack. In yet another gory scene a crocodile devoured the lower half of a pith-helmeted missionary, whose entrails spilled out from his torso as he belatedly tried to drag himself out of harm's way.

In earlier days these horrific sculptural vignettes were

installed in a trailer that Finney periodically hitched to his car and toured around the region. Decorated with hand-painted signs and murals, the mobile *CRIPIDO Museum of Horror* never failed to attract attention when he parked it alongside shopping centers and in other public locations. With the promise of a commission to the owners of these properties, he charged a small fee for the public to enter the trailer and view his "unearthly wonders" and "sanguinary scenes of human carnage."

Finney retired his traveling museum about twenty years before I met him, and he went into business with his brothers producing lawn ornaments, but he continued to create art in his spare time. His original sculptures of carved and painted plaster featured evocative images of demons, sirens, and other menacing or alluring characters, like mythological beings with cartoonishly exaggerated features. Some of them were housed with his earlier dioramas in the "FANTASTIC ART" building.

Alas, Finney willfully escaped the art dragnet Roger and I cast when we were assembling "Southern Visionary Folk Artists." I begged him to let us borrow two or three of his pieces for the exhibition, but he was firmly resistant. He was pleasant and easy to talk with, but utterly unwilling to let any of his creations out of his sight.

Months later, when I took Mitch and Angie to meet him, Finney showed us two recent sculptures, one of which he said was almost ready to be painted. The other one, complete and fully painted, was an erotically charged, columnar form that suggested a tree trunk fused together from green-skinned human and animal body parts. A repulsive, squirrel-like creature with a fanged-vulva mouth crept up the trunk toward a crowning nest suggestively positioned between two bare legs, and emerging from which was a blood-drenched maw with prominent teeth. Perched atop this ghastly organic tower, an intent-looking vulture thrust its beak into the gory mouth as if feeding it, feeding from it, or both.

"Wow!" Mitch exclaimed. "That's really nightmarish. You must have a lot of nightmares."

"Naw," Finney grinned, "I've never had a nightmare. I wish I could!"

Then, as we all continued to examine the piece, he said, "That's the whole story of life in that one right there. The whole story."

He was still putting the finishing touches on the other sculpture he showed us—a pyramidal heap of naked, emaciated, hairless human bodies, creepily reminiscent of World War II photographs documenting piled-up corpses in Nazi concentration camps. These miniature figures were crumpled as if lifeless and loosely heaped one atop another, like so much refuse in a garbage dump. A lone figure on one side of the pyramid stuck his head out and stared into space. Finney would eventually paint all these figures in a glossy, sickly shade of yellow, but on the day of our visit they remained unpainted—pristine and snowy white.

Observing our awestruck faces as we inspected the latter piece, momentarily speechless, he humbly commented, "Ain't that a mess!"

13. MOMENTOUS MEETINGS

"The Funless Eighties," Jonathan had christened our decade. With Ronald Reagan beginning a second term in the White House and rising alarm about AIDS, the designation seemed increasingly apt. Nonetheless, it would prove to be an upbeat era in the Jargon Society's history, thanks to an unforeseen confluence of factors involving culture and/or chance.

Nineteen eighty-five marked a turning point, bringing with it a veritable whirlwind of activity in our little alternative universe.

My projects on EOM and Finster were in the works, so I was making regular trips to Georgia to see both artists. These excursions always entailed overnight stops in Atlanta, Athens, and/or other points of interest in the state where I grew up, allowing time with friends and associates, and occasionally my parents.

In February, soon after our exhibition came down, I rented a big, white Chevrolet station wagon and loaded the back of it with art we'd shown. I spent a week returning pieces to their owners and having adventures along the way.

In Athens I stopped by Jerry Ayers' house on a springlike morning when I was en route to Pasaquan with some of EOM's work. Jerry proved to be an ideal traveling companion for that particular day's errand. We kept up an open-ended conversation about subjects of mutual interest and things we saw along the roadside. With its many abandoned farmhouses surreally overgrown by kudzu or purple-blooming wisteria, the rural landscape between I-85 and Saint EOM's place felt like haunted terrain.

Eddie was his usual imposing self, decked out in a yellow turtleneck and a zigzag-patterned Mexican vest with a broad-brimmed, straw hat covering the long, silver-gray hair piled on top of his head. EOM's assistant Scotty Steward helped Jerry and me unload the painted-concrete Pasaquoyan bust from the back of the station wagon. Wrapped in a blanket and several layers of foam rubber secured with duct tape, it was the heaviest piece I'd been carrying. We carefully returned it to its customary spot in the front room, reserved for Eddie's meetings with psychic-reading clients.

Scotty went back to whatever he'd been doing in another part of the compound while Jerry joined Eddie and me at our customary spot—the cluttered round table in the center of Pasaquan's exotic kitchen alcove, with its multicolored tropical-paradise murals half-hidden by the cabinets, stove, and other appliances. I rolled a joint that the three of us passed around until it was gone.

EOM was charmed by Jerry, whom he prodded for

details about his years in New York, little more than a decade after Eddie had concluded his own thirty-year residency in the city. The two of them had led parallel lives in different segments of the twentieth century. Had they been closer in age they might have shared friends in common from the demimonde.

"A wonderful old Rabelaisian character," Jerry said as we exited the driveway onto the blacktop road. We rode along in silence for a long time. Jerry was clearly moved by his encounter with Eddie Owens Martin.

With the rental car's art load lightened, we returned by way of Atlanta, where Michael Stipe was spending a couple of days for some reason I forget. We had arranged to meet him for an early dinner at Eat Your Vegetables in Little Five Points. The table conversation centered mainly on Pasaquan, which Michael said he was eager to see.

From there I drove the three of us downtown, where we met up with Kevin Miller—a Winston-Salem musician who'd relocated to Atlanta. Scrawny and wild-eyed, with long teased-out hair, he wore thrift-store clothes that he'd customized to look like an Elizabethan theatrical costume. He and Jerry could have been performers in the same troupe. Kevin and I had traveled in the same circles for a few years, but it was our first meeting. We spent a few minutes at the wreck of a loft where he was living rent-free, then we all went to the Plaza Theater to see

The Cotton Club, Francis Ford Coppola's new film about gangsters, stage performers, and flappers in Depression-era Harlem—a subculture Saint EOM had known firsthand.

It was almost midnight when the station wagon's engine quit on a four-lane stretch of U.S. Highway 78 about halfway back to Athens. I'd been so absorbed in the day's events that I hadn't even glanced at the gas gauge, which showed an empty tank. Had I needed someone or something to blame, there was the weed I'd smoked at Pasaquan, but that had been hours earlier.

Fortunately we were carrying the blankets I'd used to insulate the art in transit. They kept Jerry warm while he napped in the car and I walked to the nearest exit. I paid a convenience-store employee five bucks to drive me back to the car with a gallon can of gasoline.

When we finally got back to Jerry's house in the wee hours he invited me in so he could give me a book he'd been telling me about—*The Little Disturbances of Man*, short stories by Grace Paley.

*

In early March I drove to McLean, Virginia, for Jonathan's fifty-sixth birthday party at Ranleigh Manor, home of Doctor John Harbert, a nuclear-medicine physician and art patron. It was my second time at his house, which looked like George Washington's Mount Vernon, and the first time for Deb Coffin, who accompanied me from North Carolina.

The party was memorable for several reasons. One of the attendees was an artist I admired, William Christenberry—the Alabama landscape photographer, sculptor, and painter—who lived in nearby D.C. Likewise preceded by reputation was Ernie Mickler, *White Trash Cooking* author, whom I was meeting for the first time. He'd flown in for the occasion from his home in Florida to prepare a "Grand Canyon Cake," a massive confection in multicolored layers, drenched in whiskey sauce. The recipe was in the forthcoming cookbook.

Picture Tennessee Ernie Ford, smaller in stature and campier in demeanor, with his dark hair blond-streaked. That was Ernie Mickler, more or less, a lively, amusing, loquacious character who proudly embraced the "white trash" culture he claimed as his own. A culinary artist by profession, he'd spent years collecting recipes from friends and acquaintances who shared his cultural origins. Ernie had studied art at Mills College, and his down-to-earth photographs were icing on the proverbial cake, as distinct from the party's geologically themed, deluxe dessert—the literal cake.

Also on hand was Ranleigh's artist-in-residence Bill Dunlap, a Mississippi-born, classically trained landscape painter and muralist who said he wouldn't deny having a few white-trash roots. Bill was an amusing raconteur and longtime friend of JW. Known to me from the previous visit, he talked faster than anyone else I'd ever met from my parents' home state.

Besides introducing me to his own work, Bill had shown me a group of industrial-sandstone sculptures by a visionary artist new to me at the time, and younger than most such artists I knew—Lonnie Holley of Birmingham, Alabama. I looked at them again during this latest visit and showed them to Deb, thinking to myself that we should have included some of them in our exhibition.

*

Although "Southern Visionary Folk Artists" was organized as a one-time deal, we received invitations to reprise it at venues both far-flung and close to home, so I proceeded to organize a scaled-down version for touring. Ray Kass and I collaborated on the first such show, in Blacksburg at Virginia Tech, where Ray taught. He and a couple of his students transported the art from Winston-Salem, and I drove up into the Blue Ridge for the opening reception in early March.

The second week of April found me in Georgia again, primarily for various goings-on in Athens. On my birthday, April tenth, I attended the opening reception for a show at the University of Georgia's Tate Student Center. A young artist I knew, Chris Slay, was showing small, glass-encased photographs of road-killed wildlife, and former UGA art student Michael Stipe was exhibiting compact sculptures made from wood embellished with ink, paint, and found objects. One or two other artists may have also been included in the show, which downplayed authorship.

Photocopied flyers for this "R. Door Exhibition" incorporated old-fashioned rubber-stamp images and hand-lettered texts, e.g., *"The vivid portrayal of that around us CANNOT be left only to the professional…."*

The show also included a display of cigarettes, green apples strung from the ceiling, collages made from fast-food logos, beanbag ashtrays, a snuff can, a pedestal-mounted bag of coffee, hand-decorated balsa-wood pencil boxes, and glass laboratory slides inscribed with more hand-lettered texts, alternately obscure or mundane.

The opening reception was crowded with friends, family members, and hangers-on. Likewise an after-party hosted by a local character known as Rick the Printer.

*

Among its other unique features, Athens was home to Graphic Composition, the typography company Jonathan Williams had been using for Jargon books in recent years. My April visit coincided with the due date for page proofs of Jargon's next major publication, Lorine Niedecker's collected poems. Jonathan drove down the mountain with Tom Meyer to look them over. They arrived in town a few days after the art-show opening, and I joined them for dinner at a local Mexican restaurant. At Jonathan's invitation, I brought some friends, namely Michael Stipe, Jerry Ayers, and Kate Pierson of the B-52s.

I was quietly wondering if Kate and/or Michael might be good for some kind of contribution to our Folk Art Project—maybe a benefit concert or two. It had also occurred to me that Saint EOM's Pasaquan would be an ideal location for a music video by either of their bands. I had mentioned these idle thoughts to Jonathan, who knew little about R.E.M. or the B-52's, other than what I'd told him and the music samples I played for him. The little dinner party was his opportunity to size these kids up.

The six of us sat around a long table, with at least two conversations going on at any given moment. Jonathan's mention of his regular travels with Tom to northern England prompted Kate to recall that she'd lived in the region during an earlier phase of her life, while working as a barmaid in Newcastle. Which prompted Jonathan to inquire if she knew the poetry of Basil Bunting, a Newcastle native who had returned to that part of England in his later life. Maybe she'd even poured his ale.

Like almost anyone else who might be queried on the topic, Kate was unfamiliar with Bunting's work, as were

Jerry and Michael, so Jonathan gave them a brief career synopsis.

Known for his long poem *Brigflatts*, Bunting had lived a remarkable, immensely productive life as a poet, anti-war activist, and journalist, but had fallen on hard times in his later years. An ardent fan since the late 1960s, Jonathan had been Bunting's friend and part-time neighbor in Cumbria. In the 1970s he and Allen Ginsberg led an effort to honor Bunting in the United States. Jonathan and Tom had accompanied him on a brief tour of the East Coast in 1976, when I met the great man. Since that time the Jargon Society had served as a conduit for his financial assistance.

With Pound, Zukofsky, and William Carlos Williams all gone, Jonathan figured, that left Bunting as the most important living poet in the English language.

Unbeknown to any of us until days later, Basil Bunting would take his last breath within a few hours of that exchange.

14. "I'VE BEEN THERE,
I KNOW THE WAY"

My first successful grant-writing effort on Jargon's behalf was an appeal to the Winston-Salem-based Z. Smith Reynolds Foundation, named for tobacco tycoon R.J. Reynolds' youngest son, a precocious bon vivant who flew airplanes for a hobby. Zachary Smith Reynolds was shot to death in 1932, at the tender age of twenty, under eternally murky circumstances at the family mansion.

Fifty-three years later Roger and I gave a presentation on the Southern Visionary Folk Art Preservation Project for the ZSR Foundation's board. In the spring of 1985 they awarded us $10,000.

In early May I returned to Blacksburg for several events Ray Kass had coordinated. An exhibition of John Menapace's photographs opened in the gallery at Virginia Tech, where copies of his Jargon book were on sale. The show provided the backdrop for Jonathan's reading from his book *Blues & Roots/Rue & Bluets: A Garland for the Appalachians*, newly re-issued by Duke University Press. This event was followed by a five-day art workshop that Howard Finster conducted for students and other interested parties.

Intrigued by what he'd seen of Finster's work in our exhibition and elsewhere, Ray had made several trips to Paradise Garden in the intervening months before arranging the workshop—or "workout," as Finster insisted on calling it. Instead of holding the sessions at the university, Finster encamped at art patron Miles Horton's studio on the shore of Mountain Lake, a fifty-acre natural lake north of Blacksburg. He brought a bunch of the cutout plywood templates he customarily used to create multiples of his work, and he made them available to the students. Together they produced a series of collaborative paintings and other pieces incorporating poured concrete and salvaged materials—more than 100 works in all.

Finster's appearance attracted fans and collectors from far and near. One day he and his students were joined for a few hours by none other than L-15, who lived nearby as remote outposts go. Having heard and read so much about Finster, he presumably wanted to meet him. Schatz—I mean L—was uncharacteristically deferential, making no effort to compete for attention, as he normally might have done.

*

Late in the month I drove over to the Research Triangle to confer with Roger Manley, and to attend an R.E.M. show. Michael Stipe and his bandmates were headlining a day-long benefit concert at Meredith College in Raleigh, to raise funds for food and medical relief in sub-Saharan

Africa. The venue was an outdoor amphitheater, and most of the acts were local indy-rock bands. Perfect spring weather favored all manner of outdoor activities.

Roger and I arrived at Meredith in time to stop by the R.E.M. bus, where I introduced Roger to Michael. The band had interrupted a tour break at home in Athens to drive up to North Carolina for the day's concert. In the framed slot directly above the windshield was the phrase "*NO ONE U KNOW.*" We found Michael in an affable mood, seemingly glad to talk with us about something other than R.E.M.

I had mentioned to Roger my notion of an R.E.M. benefit show for our Folk Art Project—an idea I'd already planted in Michael's head. I didn't say anything more to him about it that afternoon, but I was encouraged that the band was playing another benefit show. Maybe our efforts weren't as noble as protecting the environment or preventing starvation in Africa, but I knew Michael was supportive. Our brief conversation on the bus that afternoon brought him up to date on our project, and his interest was further piqued by a visit the next day to Roger's house full of art, not to mention the bear skeleton in the middle of the living room.

In the meantime, R.E.M. put in an outstanding performance to close out the day. Obviously relaxed and loose after their tour break, they played for almost two hours—more than twenty songs, including a few new ones and several encores. They wound up the proceedings after dark with an especially raucous version of "Gardening at Night."

Several hours later members of R.E.M. and other bands from the Meredith show joined fans and peers at a Raleigh club called the Brewery. On the bill were local favorites the Flat Duo Jets opening for the Circle Jerks, a famous punk band from Los Angeles.

At the bar between sets I spoke briefly with R.E.M. guitarist Peter Buck. He remarked on the big white cross imprinted on the front of my black t-shirt and wondered if it had anything to do with white-cross speed. I told him I didn't know, that I'd bought the shirt in a thrift store. I noted that it could also be read as a big plus-sign.

I told Peter I'd never sampled white-cross speed. He recommended it, but he didn't offer me any.

*

With the release of their *Little Creatures* LP on June tenth, Talking Heads became the second famous rock band to creatively align themselves with Howard Finster. In Finster's commissioned cover painting, singer-songwriter David Byrne assumed the role of Atlas, holding the world on his shoulders while kneeling in the midst of a visionary landscape.

Like Michael Stipe, Byrne was a former art student,

also early on the scene as a collector of outsider art, as he liked to call it. The Atlas image was based on a self-portrait motif Finster had standardized in one of the plywood cutouts he'd brought to Mountain Lake.

Following up on R.E.M.'s use of Finster's work, *Little Creatures* helped introduce Finster to countless young music fans and musicians. Before the year was out, hordes of these indy-rock fans would join legions of university art students and adventurous collectors descending on Paradise Garden to meet the artist, listen to his ongoing monolog, and buy his paintings as fast as he could turn them out.

Thus did Howard Finster attain something akin to rock-star status, becoming an unlikely culture hero in the zeitgeist of the 1980s.

Released on the same date as *Little Creatures*, R.E.M.'s third LP *Fables of the Reconstruction* wasn't packaged with any of Finster's art, but Finster's spirit loomed over the project. One of the songs, written by Jerry Ayers, was about a neighbor of Finster's ("Old Man Kensey"). Another, "Can't Get There from Here," referenced Michael Stipe's friend Jeff Gilley, aka "Lawyer Jeff," and road trips to remote places in rural Georgia.

*

No one I knew had been acquainted with Howard Finster longer than Jeff Gilley. A fledgling attorney in

Athens, Jeff was a friend and former law-school classmate of my brother Hunter. He'd grown up in Summerville, just a few miles from Paradise Garden, and he lived across Grady Street from the rambling, old home Michael Stipe had recently bought after vacating his little rental house on Barber Street. Jeff shared our interest in Finster, Ruben Miller, and other visionary folk artists, and he knew about others I hadn't yet encountered.

During one of several stops I made in Athens that spring, Jeff took me and two or three other friends to Woodville, about forty miles south of Athens on Georgia Highway 77. On the outskirts of this tiny town in Greene County was the Reverend John D. Ruth's drive-in Bible park. The place was set well back from the highway and would have been hidden from passing travelers except for roughly life-size sculptures of a white horse and a trio of camels that could be spotted in the distance by sharp-eyed observers

"Reverend Ruth," as everyone called him, was a serene African American preacher whose pulpit was his pine-shaded yard, where he had spent untold hours creating the instructional outdoor display. Big numbers he'd painted on plywood slabs strategically posted along a meandering dirt driveway were intended to guide viewers through a chronological summary of the Old and New testaments as illustrated in sculptures, paintings, and hand-lettered signs.

During the guided walking tour he gave us, I was struck by a plywood painting of teenage Jesus talking to a group of wise men, illustrating an encounter described in the Gospel of Luke. Likewise outstanding were the concrete tablets and other components in a serial illustration of the world's creation, from the Book of Genesis.

The concluding piece in the series was a lopsided world globe made of scrap aluminum with the continents and bright blue seas rendered in what looked like tempera paint. Reverend Ruth had suspended it by a strand of white rubber clothesline in front of a celestial backdrop painted on another plywood slab—a black nighttime sky with white stars and a crescent moon.

To conclude our tour he invited us into his flat-roofed, brick ranch house, where he and his wife treated us to a few of their favorite hymns. Mrs. Ruth was a quietly dignified, diminutive woman with massive breasts and a black wig on the same scale. Her plaintive, high-pitched voice made a striking contrast with his own gravelly baritone, accompanied by chords he fingered on a toy electric organ.

After the interval of song, he showed us a little architectural model he'd made—a miniature replica of a white-columned antebellum plantation house. It was evidently based on a local landmark, the former home of R.M. Davidson, a leading white patriarch in the area.

"Now I'm going to show you something," Reverend Ruth told us, whereupon he begged a cigarette from one of us, then lit it. Lifting the roof, which was hinged on one side, he repeated himself to heighten the suspense:

"I'm going to show you something now."

He dropped the lit cigarette into the hollow interior, lined with fireproof sheet metal, then he lowered the roof.

Lo and behold, a little column of smoke emerged from the tiny chimney and trailed up toward the ceiling.

*

Not long after the visit with Reverend Ruth, Michael Stipe joined Jeff and me for a day trip to Pasaquan—a first for both of them. It was a gorgeous, late spring afternoon, and we allowed enough time for a leisurely visit with Saint EOM.

Michael and Jeff wandered the property making photographs while I spent some time with Eddie at the kitchen table. Before we left for the drive back to Athens, I made a couple of photographs of the occasion. EOM posed with Michael and Jeff on either side of him in one photo. The other photo shows Michael kneeling and aiming his camera at a detail in one of Pasaquan's walls.

Eddie's assistant Scotty later told me he thought Michael was with the rock band REO Speedwagon. EOM was likewise unfamiliar with R.E.M., but he understood that they were a famous group, and of course he had something to say about Michael's appearance. At the time Michael's hair was cut short and dyed blond.

"He looks kinda like Rod Stewart," Eddie observed, apparently having noticed Rod the Mod coloring his hair in a similar shade.

15. WAY OUT WEST

The most distant venue for the ad-hoc touring version of "Southern Visionary Folk Artists" was the Cochise Fine Arts Gallery in Bisbee, Arizona—a curious little town where I had previous experience. Situated in southern Arizona's Mule Mountains, Bisbee had been a stock-market center and a copper-mining town in the late nineteenth and early twentieth centuries. It went into decline for a few decades before its rediscovery by artists and poets in the post-hippie era. Hunter and I found our way to Bisbee in the early 1970s, when we were working summer factory jobs in Douglas, a nearby border town.

My most recent visit to Bisbee had been in 1983, for a low-budget reading tour of southern Arizona. Audiences there as well as in Tucson and Sierra Vista heard me read samples of my poetry and prose, including excerpts from the book I'd just begun writing on Saint EOM. Two years later the reading tour's organizer—my friend Jon Friedman—booked the abbreviated exhibition and a related slide talk I was to give about Jargon's Folk Art Project.

Jon was an abstract painter, cultural-events promoter, and co-founder of the widely acclaimed Bisbee Poetry Festival. He and I knew each other from Atlanta, where he spent a couple of years as an arts administrator. In

December 1984 he visited North Carolina with his wife
Shani and their young son Justin, ostensibly to see Shani's
parents near Charlotte. Our big exhibition was about to
be installed when Jon drove up to Winston-Salem for a
day, so I was able to show him a lot of the work in storage.
I also drove him out into the countryside to meet James
Harold Jennings—"an artist's artist," Jon pronounced
him.

Excited by what he'd seen, Jon returned to Bisbee and
networked with local contacts to present a version of the
show there. Together we produced a budget for shipping
and a modest lecture fee. I chose a group of works that
could be sent to Arizona with relative ease and at low
cost. Excluded of course were pieces already returned to
the artists and other lenders. Unfortunately this meant
everything from the Lynch collection and some choice
pieces I'd taken back to Georgia.

Instead of the twenty-two artists in our Winston-Salem
show—which included more than 200 pieces—the Bisbee
version consisted of about forty works by eleven artists. A
reception was scheduled for the weekend of July twelfth,
during which I was to also give my slide talk in a nearby
auditorium.

Jon met me at the airport in Tucson on the eleventh.
I planned an extended stay in order to spend more time
with him and his family before making my way east to

Roswell, New Mexico. I had been invited to visit the home of Jargon patron and board member Don Anderson.

For my lecture in Bisbee I showed slides I'd made of vernacular environments and other works by visionary folk artists, mostly in Georgia. I augmented my own photos with some of Roger Manley's images of North Carolina artists and environments. I talked extemporaneously and answered questions from the audience.

On the following day, a Sunday, I joined Jon for a road trip, ostensibly to see the artist Fritz Scholder in the hills outside Scottsdale, Arizona. Jon's seven-year-old son Justin was out of school for summer vacation, so he came along for the ride.

During a visit to the Friedmans' home earlier that year, Scholder had coveted a Victorian death wreath Jon showed him. Braids from the long, dark hair of a woman who died young, around the turn of the century, were symmetrically looped, gathered, and knotted in floral forms around a cameo photograph of her embalmed corpse, and the entire memorial assemblage was sealed under glass in an antique frame.

Scholder had offered to trade one of his own original works for the death wreath. Our day-trip mission was to visit his home, where Jon would deliver the wreath and select a piece for the swap.

The motivation behind Scholder's special interest in

the morbidly sentimental artifact became clear when we arrived at his lavish home in the desert hills above Scottsdale. His obsession with death was front and center from the moment we stepped inside.

From a broad courtyard we entered a mostly dark room whose dominant furnishing was a big, elegantly crafted, ebony desk with its empty surface smooth as polished glass. A hidden light source eerily illuminated a naked woman sprawled on the black carpet in front of the desk. Her pallid flesh was marked by cuts and bruises. She appeared to be unconscious and perhaps dead. Startling in her uncanny verisimilitude, she was in fact a work of art by the hyperrealist sculptor Duane Hanson. Once you took your eyes off this creepy necrophiliac fantasy there were many other objects to be noticed, all with the same theme.

Especially shocking were the blackened, embalmed remains of an infant in a tiny sarcophagus lying open on a cleanly designed table. It was one of several ancient mummies Scholder had acquired in Egypt with full permission from the government, he claimed. Other specimens from this officially sanctioned trove were displayed elsewhere in the house. The skin of a giant crocodile covered the floor of one large room.

After showing us his studio and an adjoining room where his prints were archived, Scholder took Jon aside so they could conduct their business in private. Justin tagged along, while I stayed behind to roam and inspect the death's-head masks, polished human bones, and mortuary artifacts from around the world. Eventually the two artists settled on a trade—the death wreath for a signed and numbered Scholder print of Jon's choice. Comparable works by Scholder were routinely selling in the mid-four-figure range at the time, Jon later told me.

On the way back we stopped in Tucson to see Chico MacMurtrie, a young Bisbee native then enrolled at Cal Arts in Los Angeles. Jon had introduced me to Chico two years earlier when he was still a promising high-school art student. This time we found him between school terms, living in a small, cheap rental house, and experimenting with sound. His latest efforts involved heavy-duty, industrial cardboard tubes of a kind normally used to support huge rolls of carpet or paper. He was using them for vocal amplification and as percussion instruments that transformed and projected any sound made on or through them, as he demonstrated while we sat on his front porch. I liked his playful, enthusiastic, anything-goes approach. He seemed destined for a significant career.

By mid-morning the next day, Monday, I was back on the road with Jon and Justin, this time headed to the Andersons' compound in Roswell. It was a long drive, about 400 miles, and we made only one extended stop, at a hot spring in the desert about one-third of the way to Roswell.

The property was private, owned by a big mining company, but Jon had been there on previous occasions and said it was rarely if ever checked by security guards. He parked at a locked metal gate that was easy to scramble under, and we walked up a low hill, the highest point for miles around. A constant flow of steaming water emerged from the earth at several spots, where stones and mortar had been used to create immersive bathtubs.

The water was at its hottest at the top of the hill, Jon explained, and slightly cooler in each of these stone-lined tubs as it flowed downhill. He and Justin removed most of their clothes and lowered themselves into one of these steaming pools about midway down. They encouraged me to do likewise, so I tested the water with my right hand. Shouting a swear-word, I jerked it back and stared at it for a moment, fully expecting the flesh to melt off.

"My God! "That's excruciatingly hot! No way am I getting in that water!"

Submerged to their bare shoulders, Jon and Justin both just looked up at me and laughed.

*

Late in the afternoon we reached Don and Sally Anderson's house in the high plains of southeastern New Mexico. The place was a kind of midcentury-modern folly that had undergone a series of idiosyncratic additions including catwalks, spiral stairs, and an architecturally eclectic, multi-story tower. Its white-painted interior was designed to catch and reflect optimum light during the day, the better to show off the art that filled every room. Large windows let in ample light and provided sweeping views of the desert.

There was art on display in all directions, but the most conspicuous piece inside the house was a larger-than-life, fiberglass sculpture by Mexican-American artist Luis Jimenez. The subject was a cowboy on horseback lassoing a massive, muscular bull that looked like it was about to rocket into space: Frederick Remington on MDA. This jaw-droppingly garish work occupied a central spot in the living room, with its cathedral ceiling open to the upstairs hallways.

The most remarkable thing on the premises, though, was a separate structure behind the house and nearly as big. Crowned by an asymmetrical configuration of massive concrete slabs that appeared to be strategically stacked a la Stonehenge, this neatly clipped, grass-covered, three-story mound paid visual homage to monuments from fallen civilizations and lost cultures. *The Henge*, it was called—an elaborately imaginative Hobbit-hole of a subterranean bomb shelter, designed for the Andersons in the late 1960s by artist Herb Goldman.

The best part was the interior, where the realist painter Willard Midgette had created striking *trompe-l'oeil* murals featuring life-size portraits of himself, Don, and the members of both their families, not to mention Jonathan Williams, who originally introduced artist and patron. From the inner sanctum of this wonderfully strange edifice a series of walkways and staircases led up to the top.

Like most of the other artists represented in Don's personal collection, both Goldman and Midgette had participated in the artist-in-residence program Don founded in 1967 and continued to bankroll under the auspices of the Roswell Museum and Art Center.

A specially designed compound near the Andersons' home provided housing and studio space for artists who spent year-long residencies in the program. Generous stipends for living expenses, supplies, and materials were provided, and there were no requirements for teaching or creative production.

Midgette was one of the program's first artists, and he became a valued advisor to Don in setting up the parameters and choosing other artists. He and his wife Sally developed a close friendship with Don and Don's wife Pat in the years before both Willard Midgette and Pat Anderson died in unrelated circumstances during the same year, 1978.

Don and Sally were married two years later, and all of this was past history by the time I met the two of them.

The Andersons were unpretentious, attentive, and deeply engaged with their enthusiasms. I related to them on the basis of our mutual interests in art and artists, so we got along very well and enjoyed each other's company. I hadn't realized until I visited his home that Don was himself an artist, a technically adept painter of imaginary landscapes whose starkly illuminated, treeless mountains struck me as metaphors for the farther reaches of his own mind.

On the morning after we arrived, Don gave us a tour of the artists' compound and introduced us to a few of the resident artists. Jon and Justin headed out from there for the long drive back to Bisbee, while I remained in Roswell for several more days. On my second night at the Andersons' I reprised the slide lecture I'd given in Bisbee, this time for members of the Roswell Museum and Art Center, assorted museum staffers, and artists from the compound—no more than fifty people.

During my time with Don I talked with him about the Folk Art Project and emphasized Roger Manley's value to our efforts. Noting the recent expiration of Roger's term as a visiting artist with the North Carolina public schools, I told Don I was concerned that his next job would divert his energy. After discussing it with me for a few minutes,

Don said he would give the Jargon Society $10,000 designated for Roger's consulting fee for one year.

At another point during my visit the conversation turned to Corn Close, the restored sheep-farmer's cottage Don owned in the Cumbrian dales of England—where Jonathan Williams and Tom Meyer were ensconced at that very moment. I'd only been in England once, with a student tour group passing through London for a few days during my teens.

For all practical purposes, Don pointed out, Corn Close was the Jargon Society's U.K. headquarters. As Jargon's executive director, he declared, I ought to visit the place. Jonathan and Tom would be in residence until late October, and Don proposed to pay my expenses for a round-trip in the meantime.

"You'll need at least a week on the ground in England," he insisted. "Make the arrangements, and I'll reimburse Jargon for your plane ticket and any other costs. Let Jonathan and Tom know when you'll be there. They love entertaining visitors, and I'm sure they'll be delighted to have you with them."

16. SURREALITY CHECK

My return from the Southwest marked the end of my first year in Winston-Salem, an anniversary of mostly personal significance, but one that coincided with several important developments for the Jargon Society.

I had finished the manuscript for my book on Saint EOM, representing two years of interviews and untold hours of writing, tape-transcription, and editing. I asked EOM to fact-check it and let me know if he wanted to change anything. He complimented my accuracy but questioned my decision to let his voice carry the story. I think he'd envisioned a dramatization with an omniscient narrator, but I tried to convince him his firsthand account was unsurpassable.

Some readers would be shocked by EOM's vivid language and graphic details about his salacious escapades in New York, I figured, and I hoped this wouldn't render our goal of preserving Pasaquan more difficult. Such was the concern expressed by a few people I allowed to read the manuscript. Cautionary comments notwithstanding, I felt that any effort to sanitize Eddie's story would mute his feisty spirit and diminish the narrative's power.

By early August a copy of the manuscript was in the mail to Jonathan at Corn Close.

Meanwhile, commerce threatened to impinge on

EOM's self-made world. As we learned not a moment too soon, a multi-national paper company planned to clearcut the woods surrounding Eddie's property.

An essential part of the charm and drama of Pasaquan was its secluded setting. It was concealed behind the low-growth pines and dwarf oaks until you got right up on it. Clearcutting it would ruin the effect and render the site physically vulnerable. We couldn't let it happen.

I wrote to the president of the Buckeye Cellulose Corporation, suggesting a tax-deductible contribution of ten acres as a buffer zone around Pasaquan. He countered with an offer to sell the land for $750 an acre. The last thing I needed was an obligation to raise another $7,500, so I pressed on with my effort toward a donation.

There was no more authoritative figure in southwest Georgia than former President Jimmy Carter. I didn't know him personally, but Eddie did. Carter had visited Pasaquan in the 1960s, and other members of the Carter family had been paying clients for Eddie's "psychic readings." So I wrote to the former President requesting a letter of support, as a nudge of encouragement for the paper company to do the right thing. Our effort to forestall the clearcut threat would prove to be an enduring drama, dragged out through the late 1980s.

*

The first week of August '85 found me on the road with

Roger Manley, visiting artists in eastern North Carolina. Newly informed of Don Anderson's offer to retain his services for the next year, Roger was relieved, so the mood was light. He laughingly declared us "Raiders of the Lost Art."

Roger and I got along remarkably well and shared many of the same interests and enthusiasms, although we came at them from different angles. The only subject we disagreed on was jazz, which Roger couldn't abide because it made him nervous, he told me. Nor could Roger smoke pot if he was going to drive anywhere, because under the influence of cannabis he lost all sense of direction. Not a problem for me, although I let him drive while I gazed out the windows and sometimes smoked.

Our first stop out of Durham was the wondrous Occoneechee Trapper's Lodge, alongside the highway in front of Quinton J. Stephenson's house in Northampton County. QJ, as everyone called him—Robert Lynch's white boy—had made some of the most strikingly weird sculptures in our exhibition. We showed up at his house unannounced and found no one home, but his little lodge was unlocked and fully accessible. It was the most exotic sight for miles around, and yet it was entirely made of things QJ had found within a day's drive of the place.

A compact, one-room structure hand-built of stones, logs, and stucco, the lodge was ornamented with hundreds

of natural and man-made objects from the forests and
swamps QJ had spent his life exploring. Fossilized sea
creatures, Indian arrowheads, animal bones, unusual
rocks, oddly shaped wood forms, Civil-War relics,
and antique bottles were embedded in the surfaces
and conjoined to form some of the more idiosyncratic
architectural features. QJ had incised explanatory and
interpretive texts into some of the concrete slabs, not
unlike wall texts you might see in a natural-history
museum. We spent an hour making photographs and
waiting in vain for him to return.

Later that afternoon we found William Owens at his
house near Currituck Sound, albeit with very little of his
art on hand, and not a piece for sale. I was glad to meet
Owens, an amiable, utterly unassuming but anxious-
seeming fellow—wiry and long of neck, with freckled
skin the color of cream-splashed coffee. I'd been hoping
to buy one of his painted bathing-beauty sculptures, but
the handful of finished pieces in evidence were already
promised to other collectors who'd paid for them in
advance, he told us. During the hour we spent with him
he seemed perplexed and a little depressed.

From Owens' house we headed south to the Outer
Banks and the tiny island town of Buxton, where I finally
got to meet Annie Hooper. Just as I'd been told, every
room of her house was filled with her biblical sculptures,

leaving just enough clearance for narrow passageways.

A tiny, birdlike woman whose clothing complemented her white hair and milky skin, Ms. Hooper seemed to give off a phosphorescent glow. She greeted us warmly, and she treated Roger like a grandson. She'd recently been featured in the *Durham Morning Herald*—a full-page article illustrated with one of his photographs. Handing him a copy, she pointed and—in an almost childlike voice—declared, "I look like a spook in that picture, Roger. I ought to spank your bottom and break that camera!"

We spent the night in a nearby rental cottage Ms. Hooper's family owned, although they refused to charge us a dime. The next day we rode two ferries—the first to Ocracoke Island, then a much larger one across a very choppy Pamlico Sound—back to the mainland.

Resuming our seats in Roger's van, we cruised into Belhaven, North Carolina, home of the singularly eclectic Belhaven Memorial Museum. Headquartered on the upper floor of an old firehouse in the center of this little town on the Pungo River, the museum contained the lifetime collection of Eva Blount Way, a local eccentric rumored to have operated a house of ill repute. Whatever else she did with her time, and however she came by her collection, Ms. Way had spent the first half of the twentieth century acquiring all manner of curious objects. On her death in the early 1960s she bequeathed it all to her hometown.

The holdings of the 7,700-square-foot firehouse loft included a whale's rib, a mummified squirrel, a stuffed peacock, a rattlesnake-hide necktie, a ten-pound fibroid tumor, more than 30,000 buttons, a 1909 Edison gramophone, a German machine gun from World War One, a nineteenth-century ship's anchor, a spittoon that looked like a turtle, a fragment of a NASA spacecraft, a pair of petrified walrus tusks, a custom-made dress for a 700-pound woman, a soccer ball-sized ball of twine, a collection of dead fleas dressed for a wedding, a Seminole Indian chief's patch-quilted jacket, a dead snake disfigured by the wooden egg it had swallowed, a map of Vietnam made of multicolored drinking straws, an array of discontinued household products, and shelves lined with jars of pickled human fetuses and deformed animal embryos.

*

It was an ideal way to make a living—visiting people like Annie Hooper and places like the Belhaven Memorial Museum and the Occoneechee Trapper's Lodge, photographing them and writing about them. But how long could it last? Even the three years I'd been promised didn't seem likely. Dark clouds loomed on Jargon's financial horizon.

The society's fiscal year began on July first, and mid-August found us nearly as broke as we'd been in January.

The funds from the Z. Smith Reynolds Foundation were gone, and my efforts to raise additional money had so far come to naught. While we awaited word on pending foundation grants to the tune of $28,000, we were spending $5,000 a month, and we'd only taken in half that much all summer, including book sales and contributions. The foundation named for Philip's uncle, James G. Hanes, declined my application for $10,000 to support the Folk Art Project. Foundation chairman J. Gordon Hanes Jr. didn't like the mention of a possible museum.

"The last thing Winston-Salem needs is another museum," he groused. "We can barely support the museums we have."

Gorgon, as Jonathan liked to call him, wasn't one to mince words. A snide personal comment about a family member had evidently been Jonathan's final, fatal offense as far as Gordon was concerned. Lacking the diplomatic skills to mediate such enduring grudges between my elders, I had to let it lie.

Gordon Hanes was in fact an exceptional character, a peerless patron of visual art in North Carolina, likewise a supporter of progressive politics at home, including the local chapter of the Black Panther Party. He made a token personal contribution of $100 to Jargon that year, but his foundation declined our grant request.

Meanwhile, Ernie Mickler's forthcoming recipe-and-photo book seemed to promise some future income, but Jargon's track record discouraged any such expectations. *White Trash Cooking* was still in production and had been plagued with cost overruns and printing delays, much to the consternation of Philip Hanes, who threatened to rescind his $10,000 publication loan if he couldn't be assured of having copies for friends on his Christmas list.

With all these fires to be put out, Jargon's executive committee was convened in early September. Don and Sally flew in from New Mexico, and—since his new consulting assignment was one of the matters up for discussion—Roger Manley drove over from Durham. Locals in on this exclusive pow-wow included Philip Hanes, Borden Hanes, and Ted Potter.

Bottom line: Disaster was averted thanks largely to Don, who delivered the promised check for Roger's fee and made another substantial loan toward *White Trash Cooking*.

Not to be completely outdone, and despite his previous threat to withdraw his loan, Philip pitched in another $1,000 toward the book's production, as did his attorney nephew Borden. By the meeting's end we calculated Jargon could afford to publish 5,000 copies of Ernie's book.

Meanwhile, money being so tight, I had quietly given up on the idea of going to England. But after bailing Jargon out again, Don reminded me about his offer to pay for the trip. Jonathan and Tom were scheduled to return to the states in late October, he noted.

"So you'd better get over there soon!"

17. IDYLL IN DENTDALE

After consulting Jonathan I booked flights that would put me in England for eight days at the end of September. And so I jetted across the Atlantic for the first time in more than a decade. The long flight allowed plenty of time for reading, writing, and sleeping, although I didn't sleep much.

After navigating my way through Heathrow Airport I caught a cab to Hampstead—number thirteen, South Hill Park— the home of Adrian and Celia Mitchell, longtime friends of Jonathan. They had offered to put me up in London on both ends of my trip. On my first pass I would only be with them for a few hours before boarding an overnight train to Cumbria.

I found the Mitchells at home and expecting me. We got acquainted over tea, of course. I was immediately taken with their comfortable three-story row house full of books. Previously unknown to this ignorant Yank, they were established cultural figures in England—Adrian as a journalist, novelist, poet, and political activist, and Celia as a stage and film actress under her maiden name Hewitt. Jonathan had filled me in to that extent, although there was no sign of the two attractive daughters he'd mentioned.

The Mitchells' home overlooked the legendary

Hampstead Heath, where I went for a brief, solitary walk to stretch my limbs between travel intervals. I left my bag next to the Mitchells' front door. When I returned Celia showed me to a guest room, and I was able to nap for about an hour before taking a cab to Euston Station.

With the passing countryside mostly cloaked in darkness, I also slept on the train, but fitfully. My thoughts were scattered as I drifted in and out of consciousness, but at intervals my mind focused on the two friends I was on my way to see—convivial colleagues who'd come to loom large in my life.

Jonathan Williams was one of a kind, in spades. The force of his personality was like a strong wind blowing down from the mountains. He'd certainly learned from the best of big personalities—people like Charles Olson, Kenneth Rexroth, Henry Miller, and Marlene Dietrich. And there was his physical size, six-four with his shoes off. He was brilliant, opinionated, well-versed in his fields of interest, and determined in whatever he undertook. Supremely sure of himself, he was uncompromising in his lifestyle, his enthusiasms, and his personal choices. He could be and often was greatly amusing, tossing out zingers left and right.

"I'm only gay below the waist!" he once proclaimed, apropos of I can't remember what.

Raised without siblings, Jonathan remained in every

sense the ultimate only child. Self-indulgent? You bet, and wholly indifferent to anyone's disapproval. Offense was gladly provided for those who chose to take same. And yet he was one of the most generous people I'd ever known. Like his own mentors, he regarded all forms of collectivity with suspicion. His generosity, like his attention, was highly specific, focused on individuals, particular places, and singular things.

An epicurean and a determined natural aristocrat, JW had accustomed himself to the finer things. This had been apparent on our first meeting. The tailored tweed suits, expensive cigars, globe-hopping lifestyle, and the decidedly non-commercial books he managed to stylishly publish—I assumed there was a trust-fund somewhere. Not exactly the case, I later learned.

Jonathan had benefited from the hard work, ingenuity, and good fortune of his father, T. Ben Williams, who designed filing systems for federal government agencies. Daddy Ben's upward mobility enabled the Williams family to buy the forty-acre farm in North Carolina's Nantahala Mountains, where he commissioned the rustic house built for them toward the end of World War Two.

The Williamses also collected antiques, of which Jonathan's mother was a part-time dealer, through the shop she operated during tourist seasons in the upscale resort town of Highlands. Jonathan's keenly appraising eye was inherited and homebred. Unlike his father, he rarely made any money, but he had very specific ideas about how to spend it when good-old-fashioned patronage provided.

Despite Jonathan's large-living shadow, Tom Meyer was extraordinary in his own way. He was, first, a very different kind of poet. His work was more lyrical, discursive, and seemingly serious of purpose, although certainly not lacking in humor. Born and bred in Seattle, Tom was a twenty-two-year-old student at Bard College when he met Jonathan, thirty-nine. That was 1968, three years before Jargon published *The Bang Book*, a poetic tale about the Old West and legendary outlaw Wild Bill Hickok. It would be the first of Tom's many publications under many imprints.

Quickly recognizing Tom's special qualities including his physical charms, Jonathan had cultivated and mentored him. Exotic yet down to earth, Tom was diamond-bright, fun to talk with, physically super-fit, and nice to look at. He was also accomplished in more than one art. His culinary skills were already legendary by the time I got to know him. And he was the only poet I knew who kept current with fast-developing computer technology, digital graphics, and other technophilic business.

When I met them Jonathan and Tom had been together for five years. Their first mutual venture had been a trip to England in 1970 to buy a cottage for Don Anderson. I'd been hearing about Corn Close for as long as I'd known them, and I'd seen photographs that certainly made it look like a place one would want to visit.

It was broad daylight, mid-morning, when my train finally arrived at Oxenholme. The dynamic duo met me at the station in the Morris Ital station wagon Don had bought for use at Corn Close. Fondly nicknamed *foie gras*, aka FG—because it was exactly the color of goose-liver pâté, as Tom pointed out.

Dazzling green hills under slate-gray skies occasionally broken by sunlight—the landscape was as stunningly beautiful as advertised. My ancestors came from this part of the world, so maybe I was experiencing some kind of genetic resonance, but I immediately felt an uncanny sense of belonging in this place I was seeing for the first time.

Halfway between the towns of Sedbergh and Dent, along the River Dee at the lower end of Dentdale, a narrow gravel driveway climbed part-way up the steep slope of Middleton Fell, crisscrossed with ancient, moss-covered stone fences. Sheep grazing here and there on the hillside paused to cast inscrutable gazes on the whining, meat-colored machine that rolled past them with our faces peering out the windows.

At the end of the drive on the right was the 300-year-old stone cottage, dug into the hill with its front side brightly whitewashed. Immediately below it, on the lower left as we approached, was a stone barn, equally ancient, which Don had extensively renovated as a living space for his family when they were at Corn Close. So named, by the way, because the house was close to the grain storage, i.e., the corn was close, or nearby.

We entered the cottage through a heavy wooden door enclosed in a slate-roofed porch gable. A collection of walking sticks and shepherds' crooks greeted us in the entry hall as Jonathan warned me to duck so I wouldn't hit my head on the rafters—more of a hazard for him than for me.

After storing my bag in the upstairs guest bedroom I was treated to a quick tour. As solidly built as any house I'd ever set foot in, it had stone walls throughout, some of them several feet thick, and a stone floor downstairs. The walls of one room were lined with original paneling removed from a nearby Norman church, and the wooden staircase to the second floor had been salvaged from another antique building.

Redolent of cigar smoke, old wood, books, and rarified home cooking, the house smelled like Jonathan's family home in North Carolina. Other resemblances to the Skywinding house included the boldly painted woodwork in several rooms. And the art—original paintings and drawings by the likes of R.B. Kitaj, Glen Baxter, and the Furnivals, John and Astrid. There were portraits of both poets—Willard Midgette's painting of Jonathan circa 1968, dapperly attired and holding a cigar in moody chiaroscuro; and Sandra Fisher's vivid drawing of Tom languidly napping, nude in full sunlight. Also watercolors and photographs by Brits whose names I didn't recognize, and a few of Don's imaginary landscapes.

In a small room with its own fireplace was an ancient-looking folk painting of a lion, originally employed as a pub sign. Its modern-day counterpart was the life-size cardboard cutout of Colonel Harland Sanders, white-suited and string-tied, in one corner of the library—appropriated from a Kentucky Fried Chicken outlet by one or another of JW's friends.

The ample supply of books constituted another feature reminiscent of the North Carolina house. Filling high shelves built into one of the library's walls were probably 2,000 volumes of poetry, photography, and commentary on music, art, and other subjects of particular interest. Shelved on an adjoining wall were several hundred vinyl record albums that residents and visitors enjoyed hearing on the cottage's state-of-the-art sound system. Heated by a woodstove with a water-filled copper saucepan on top, the room was a cozy spot for reading or listening. The ceiling angled sharply upward to skylight windows looking out on the steeply sloping pasture with sheep grazing uphill in the distance.

A rare pleasure indeed to house at this pastoral retreat. I felt like a Tolkien character. I would have been content to remain at the cottage for my entire stay, but Jonathan had other plans, and I was happy to let him play guide. Instead of striking out on a walking tour of the dales, we set forth in FG, with JW at the wheel, Tom insisting on the back seat, and myself riding left-hand shotgun.

Our first stop on the first day out was Brigflatts Quaker Meeting House in nearby Sedbergh. From the outside it resembled a larger version of Corn Close—not surprising since the two structures were contemporaneous, probably worked on by the same local craftsmen. The oldest meeting house in the North of England, completed in 1675, Brigflatts was previously known to me only as the setting for Basil Bunting's great poem.

It was a chilly day, late morning, with no one else around. The front door was unlocked, so we ventured inside the open, two-level room with its bare plank floors, stark benches, and simple, dark-stained woodwork. I found the stairs to the second-level balcony, which looked down on the main sanctuary from three sides. We sat quietly for a few minutes, and I thought about Bunting, only five months absent from our mortal company. I'm sure Jonathan was also thinking about his old friend and colleague. He said it was the first time he'd visited Brigflatts without the local poet-sage.

Extending our Bunting-themed pilgrimage, Jonathan drove us to Dentdale and pointed out the River Dee's confluence with the Rawthey, name-checked in the opening lines of "Brigflatts."

Every day we ventured out to see other points of interest, visiting friends along the way. We dined and drank in the boys' favored pubs including the Barbon Inn in Barbondale and the Snooty Fox in Kirby Lonsdale, we drove through the Lake District, and we met up with artist Karl Torok in Bradford. We were treated to lunches, dinners, and tea in the homes of friends involved in literature and art. We spent a night with Jonathan's and Tom's friend Ronnie Duncan, a patron and collector of Ian Hamilton Finlay, in Otley, a small town near Leeds.

Throughout my visit I had the odd sensation of time's passing both slowly and swiftly, so maybe it all balanced out. In any case, I was feeling quite at home by leave-taking time.

Instead of riding the train for another thirteen hours back to London, I caught a flight from Manchester. Jonathan drove me to the airport in the morning, and I was back at the Mitchells' house by mid-afternoon. Sam Farber had recently put me in touch with Monika Kinley and Victor Musgraves, whose outsider-art collection I had hoped to visit in London, but unfortunately they weren't available during the couple of hours I had to spare. This left time for a more leisurely visit with Adrian and Celia at their charming home, again my quarters in transition.

Adrian gave me inscribed copies of his latest books—a collection of poems, *For Beauty Douglas*, illustrated by (none other than) Ralph Steadman, and a counterpart written for children, *Nothingmas Day*, with intricate woodcuts by British artist John Lawrence. In the evening I walked with Adrian and Celia to an Indian restaurant where I treated them to dinner—the least I could do to repay their hospitality in some small part.

The place was crowded, loud, and dimly lighted. The Mitchells were apparently regulars, as they received familiar greetings from the *maitre-de* and other patrons. Within minutes after we placed our orders, our table was visited by a gangly, professorial, white-haired gentleman in horn-rims and well-worn tweeds.

I tried to play down my astonishment when Celia introduced Michael Foot. *The* Michael Foot—prominent left-wing politician and former leader of Britain's Labour Party, two years out of office. I knew just enough about British politics to know who he was. It turned out he and Adrian were longtime friends from their days as fellow journalists, and he spontaneously joined us for dinner. We almost had to shout to make ourselves heard, but we managed to carry on a lively conversation about the dismal state of U.S. and British politics—Maggie Thatcher and Ronnie Ray-gun—and about art.

The right honorable Mr. Foot seemed to take a genuine interest in the Jargon Society's Folk Art Project, which I told him about with the Mitchells' encouragement. I was surprised that he was familiar with Jonathan Williams, but of course he was a literate citizen. I hadn't yet figured out that Jonathan was more widely known in the U.K. than in the U.S.A.

As I was paying the tab, our dinner companion invited us to his nearby home for a nightcap. The air was refreshing as we walked several blocks to the Foots' row-house, where the furniture was arranged to accommodate an overflow of books and newspapers, most but not all of which were neatly stacked and shelved. On a low table in the center of the living room was a vase of freshly cut flowers.

Mrs. Foot—aka Jill Craigle, documentary filmmaker—was there when we arrived, and proved to be her husband's equal as an engaging conversationalist. She showed me a lushly illustrated book about Yugoslavian folk art, apparently one of her special interests—"naive art," as it was known in the Slavic lands. How, she wondered, did I think the visionary folk art we were documenting in the American South compared with this material from eastern Europe?

A civilized evening to cap off my restorative visit to the UK. The brandy we imbibed with the Foots kept the Mitchells and me warm for the half-hour it took us to walk back to their house.

Early the following afternoon I was airborne, winging my way back to the USA and a days-long bout of bad jet lag.

Crew from MTV's "The Cutting Edge" films Jonathan Williams reading from his *Blues & Roots/Rue & Bluets* (Duke University Press edition, 1985) in the RJR/ Sawtooth Gallery, Winston-Salem, with pieces from the exhibition, "Southern Visionary Folk Artists," January 1985. Photo by Roger Manley.

Bernard Schatz, aka L-15, with "Oedipus" masks and other works, rural West Virginia, 1984. Photo by Roger Manley.

Annie Hooper with some of her biblical driftwood figures at her home in Buxton, North Carolina, 1984. Photo by Roger Manley.

Howard Finster plays his banjo, Paradise Garden, Chattooga County, Georgia, 1984. Photo by Roger Manley.

R.A. Miller on "Windmill Hill," Rabbittown, Georgia, 1984.
Photo by Tom Patterson.

Chuck Alston, aka Also Aswell, *Cosmic Raymobile*, Greensboro, North Carolina, 1984. Photo by Tom Patterson.

Michael Stipe, Deborah Coffin, Cynthia Williams, and Jerry Ayers, Winston-Salem, 1985. Photo by Tom Patterson.

James Harold Jennings (left) with Michael Stipe, Pinnacle, North Carolina, 1985. Photo by Tom Patterson.

Jerry Ayers in Winston-Salem, 1985. Photo by
Tom Patterson.

Michael Stipe at 248 Barber Street, Athens, Georgia, 1985. Photo by Tom Patterson.

Howard Finster at the grave of his elder sister Abbie
Rose Finster (1905-1919), northeast Alabama, 1987.
Photo by Tom Patterson.

Howard Finster's Paradise Garden, panorama, Chattooga County, Georgia, 1986. Photo by Roger Manley.

Howard Finster's Paradise Garden, panorama with flying angel and 'Coin Man,' Chattooga County, Georgia, 1986. Photo by Roger Manley.

Howard Finster, concrete mountain with mirror shards and generic statuary, Paradise Garden, Chattooga County, Georgia, 1986. Photo by Roger Manley.

Roger Manley (left) and Tom Patterson sign copies of *St. EOM in the Land of Pasaquan* (Jargon Society, 1987) while William Burroughs signs a *Naked Lunch* paperback edition, Elliot Bay Books, Seattle, July 1988.

William Burroughs with lemurs, Durham, North Carolina, 1989.
Photo by Tom Patterson

18. LIMBO SHOW

Early in the year my uncontested divorce from Ellen was legally processed for a minimal fee the two of us split evenly. As a personal milestone it was anti-climactic. Ellen and I continued to amiably correspond, and I invariably saw her during visits to Atlanta. We seemed to get along much better with a few hundred miles between us and our communications mostly in writing.

The little romance with Deborah had cooled by the spring. I enjoyed getting to know a French-language teacher and a metalwork artist whose names and related details are immaterial to the present account—although I will allow that one of them had twelve toes.

Ambivalent about romantic love and so-called committed relationships, I had plenty of other things to occupy my time and attention. Still, I was thirty-three, which didn't feel much different from twenty-three. On yet another hand, sex had apparently become a deadlier pursuit. One had to be careful, and so one was.

Late in the spring I met an eccentric abstract painter, exactly my age and height but slimmer and prettier. A Goldie Hawn type—leggy and naturally blond, with disarmingly big, blue eyes and a soft, breathy voice. Diana Dorn by name—no known relation to poet Ed Dorn and no resemblance to the British B-movie actress Diana Dors, although of course that's what Jonathan Williams would come to call her.

I met Diana at a party following an art-exhibition opening in Greensboro, where almost everyone in attendance lived. Well into the evening, after sending her date on his way, she asked me to drive her home, which of course I did. Since I was thirty miles from home she did the neighborly thing and invited me to spend the night. Which of course I did.

The two-story, yellow clapboard house occupied a maple-shaded yard in a residential neighborhood close to the UNC-G campus. I liked the way Diana had decorated the place—tasteful and contemporary but idiosyncratic. Clean lines, no clutter, low lighting, white blinds in the windows, and art magazines on the glass-topped coffee table, which held a cylindrical, blown-glass vase containing fresh tulips. On the cream-white walls a few framed photographs and paintings on unstretched canvases. Everything looked carefully considered, camera-ready for a photo-spread in an interior-design magazine. It was impressive and a little unnerving.

The paintings turned out to be Diana's own—abstract, glyphic symbols that suggested ancient mathematical equations, painted on scuffed, stone-like surfaces, some of which had tiny bits of computer circuitry attached. Very different from what I was used to looking at, but interesting in their way. They looked good from a distance, without regard to what they might be about, and they had a lot of surface nuance up close.

Diana had her own sense of style, and I found her amusing. Also in residence at her house were Zeno—a huge, *HUGE* Doberman/Great Dane mix, unfortunately in declining health—and Buzzy, a double yellow-headed Amazon parrot. Zeno was an upstairs-downstairs dog who found the stairs increasingly hard to negotiate. His back legs clearly weren't working like they once had, and he seemed to spend most of his time lying on the floor in Diana's upstairs bedroom.

Buzzy wasn't one of those foul-mouthed birds, but he possessed a repertoire of clever comments ("*I can talk. Can you fly?*") and non-verbal sounds that amusingly mimicked muffled human voices heard from another room—or from under the gray sheet of loose canvas Diana pulled over his big, black iron cage when she wanted him to sleep.

Klee klie klo. Klee klie klo. Klo? Klie-klo. Ah ha ha ha ha! Et cetera.

Diana's record collection was modest—maybe 100 LPs total. Grace Jones, some reggae, some jazz, and a few more anomalous selections. I was mildly astonished to find among them an album by an obscure South American jazz-rock band called Opa, which I happened to like a lot.

I asked personal questions—my usual practice when getting to know anyone. Like me, Diana was the eldest of four siblings. Her birthday was three days before mine, same year. She and her sisters and their little brother spent their childhood in the U.S. Virgin Islands during their father's stint as a psychologist with the Peace Corps. As a child she had a pet chicken named Chickodemus. When she was in her teens the family moved to Greensboro, where her dad founded a non-profit consulting business that was still extant and successful as of 1985. Her parents divorced but both stayed in Greensboro and found other partners. Her mom went to work as a librarian. Diana moved to Charlotte to study art at that city's state university branch.

A decade later she was evidently still a serious practitioner, although only marginally professional. Back in Greensboro she showed her paintings at a few local galleries and was acquainted with most of the other artists in town. She didn't have an advanced degree, so she was ineligible to teach, as some of her peers did, and she sold her work sporadically. Like other artists I knew, she performed menial jobs to support herself. Since her college days she'd had a couple of boyfriends who financially supported her in whole or in part. Nice work if you could get it, seemingly, but not guaranteed to turn out well, she allowed.

Although she initially came off as spacey and naive, Diana had certainly been around the block. She was smarter than she initially let on, and savvier than I was about contemporary art. She had about a decade's worth of *Arts* magazine shelved in chronological order, and she'd evidently read them carefully, following all the latest theoretical debates and sometimes taking sides. She talked about the writers as if she knew them.

She was a character for sure, and I found her kind of sexy despite her angularity. By the fall we had become an item.

*

It was a busy season. In early October Roger and I mounted a small exhibition from the Jargon folk-art collection at Duke University Hospital. I drove to Durham so the two of us could show it to local arts patrons and political leaders. We also toured an old church building as a possible site for a visionary folk-art museum—still a pipe dream for JW. Or a cigar dream

I made two trips to Atlanta in the last half of the month. The first was to see a group exhibition at Nexus called "Vietnam and Its Aftermath," and a related performance by participating artist L-15, whose work I had introduced to the show's curators. During his visit to Atlanta I had arranged for L-15 to spend two nights at Lucinda Bunnen's big house in Buckhead and a night at my brother Hunter's modest apartment in Peachtree Hills.

Lucinda found L-15 amusing and bought at least one of his best recent sculptures. Not Hunter. My brother was annoyed by him, he told me, because he never stopped performing. It was all part of the act—one of L-15's favorite phrases.

L-15's onstage performance at Nexus was a "new, improved" version of the "lecture" he'd given in Winston-Salem early in the year, he told me, and indeed it reprised some of the core components, including the bit about the proposed *Giant Eyeball Tower*. There was a lot of improvisational interplay with the audience, which he seemed to delight in taunting. I reviewed the event for *Art Papers*.

The second Atlanta trip was to pick up Jonathan and Tom at the airport. Having flown back from England a few days earlier, they'd proceeded to New Orleans for a symposium on the Southern surrealist photographer Clarence John Laughlin, at which Jonathan gave a talk. On their return from the Crescent City I met them at Hartsfield-Atlanta International and drove them home to Skywinding Farm, where I spent a night before proceeding on to Winston-Salem.

*

Thanks to Roger I made my debut as an exhibiting artist in November. Some of Roger's friends in Charlotte had pooled their resources to lease a decommissioned fire station as an art venue. They named it the Limbo Gallery and invited Roger to curate a show for them. Instead of pulling together another exhibition like the one he and I had organized, he simply invited friends who made anything resembling art to contribute examples for a show he titled "Off the Beaten Path." It opened on the first weekend in November, coinciding with a series of documentary-photography talks at the Light Factory, a non-profit gallery in the same part of Charlotte.

A few months earlier Roger had introduced me to the Light Factory's new director Mark Sloan—also an exhibitor in the Limbo Show—who invited me to give a talk on this program. I showed a selection of slides—including my own, Roger's, and a few by other photographers—of subjects including Saint EOM and Annie Hooper, along with examples of their work. My talk was an extemporaneous plug for the Jargon Society's Southern Visionary Folk Art Project, but I was paid a visiting lecturer's fee and expenses including overnight lodging.

There was no overriding theme for the Limbo Gallery show. The title referenced the relatively uncharted areas where Roger often made some of his most exciting art discoveries—"Off the Beaten Path." Represented were artists from his home turf (Bryant Holsenbeck, Kim

Irwin, Rodney Dickens, Khoo Su Nin), others he'd met in his near-and-far travels (Richard C., Ira DeKoven, Eugene Langford, Tom Stanley, Ed Wicklander), and people he'd met through me (David Lee, Elizabeth Lide, Stan Sharshal, Michael Stipe, Jerry Ayers, Also Aswell). It was an all-embracingly pluralistic affair, bringing together multiple mediums and engaging diverse subjects treated in an array of terminologically elusive styles. At least half of the artists had been academically trained, and none were exponents of what we called visionary folk art. In many ways it was a perfect complement to our Winston-Salem show.

My contribution was a display of materials excerpted from the personal archives I stored in a couple of old metal file cabinets. One small collage I'd made, a few found photographs, and images I had appropriated from various sources—twelve items in all, each in a clear plastic sleeve, none having any direct connection with the others. They were displayed in three rows of four, with each one clipped and hung on a tiny nail on one of three horizontal strips of black wall molding. I gave it a straightforward, descriptive title: *Items from the Files.*

To publicize the show Roger asked the artists to submit photos or other images of themselves, which he used to make a montage vaguely resembling a staged group photo. He commissioned a poster-printing company to reproduce it with the pertinent info including a list of the exhibiting artists, all on a rainbow-hued background, like the ubiquitous posters for wrestling matches, gospel-music shows, and blues concerts.

The opening reception was crowded with almost all of the represented artists, their friends and family members, and other people I'd never seen before. The audience for my talk at the Light Factory was similarly packed. Standing room only.

*

Diana accompanied me to Charlotte for those two events. By the end of the year we were living together in my tiny apartment, although she continued to rent and regularly visit her Greensboro house, which still contained most of her belongings. Sadly, she had to put her big dog Zeno to sleep, as the euphemism goes, due to a cascade of physical infirmities. She found a job waiting tables at a seafood restaurant in Winston-Salem, and after a few months was able to rent the two-story apartment that made up the rest of my house.

Buzzy was too much bird for my little apartment, so he and his big cage were temporarily installed in the kitchen at 1000 West Fifth Street, right next to the Jargon office. During his brief tenure as Jargon's mascot, Buzzy even earned a mention in a newspaper article about Jonathan's maverick press. What reporter or reader could resist an exotic, gibberish-spouting bird in the office kitchen?

Buzzy retired from this short-lived public role after Diana moved into the front apartment, where she found a spot for his cage alongside the kitchen—site of the previously referenced barking-dog episodes.

19. TRANSITION AND TRASH

R.E.M. were back in North Carolina in December, on an East-Coast tour with the Minutemen opening. A well-placed phone call got me comp tickets and backstage passes for their concerts in Raleigh (December second) and Winston-Salem (December eighth). On the afternoon of the Winston-Salem show at Reynolds High School Auditorium I picked up Michael Stipe at the downtown hotel where he was staying and drove out to see James Harold Jennings.

In the months since Michael's first visit, early in the year, Jennings' place had undergone some changes—most conspicuously a decommissioned school bus diagonally parked at the back edge of the clearing where Jennings displayed his art. Jennings had also been creating ever more elaborate "art worlds," as he called them—sprawling assemblages of painted cut-out wood that couldn't be missed from the road. These creations were typically dismantled piecemeal as collectors bought parts of them, except for one that was later purchased in its entirety and hauled off on a flatbed truck.

Jennings used proceeds from his escalating art sales to buy the bus at an auction, but he never intended to use it for transportation. Instead he arranged for it to be parked in situ as a kind of multi-purpose storage unit and shelter. At some point its original yellow exterior had been overpainted with white. After it was stationed in long-term parking he filled it with art supplies and materials along with books and magazines he'd carried across the road from the old homeplace, which he'd seemingly abandoned. He removed a couple of seats and contrived a space for a sleeping pallet, and he installed a compact, wood-burning stove for use in exceptionally cold weather.

Jennings had mixed feelings about his art's increasing popularity. He delighted in showing off the business cards left by visitors who bought his art, and he seemed especially proud of its appeal to doctors, lawyers, and other high-level professionals, whose credentials were typically noted on the cards.

On the other hand he complained about the growing demands on his production. As his work became more widely known, collectors began requesting new treatments of favored subjects, including angels, airplanes, cats, birds, celestial bodies, and Indians wearing feathered headdresses.

Michael didn't buy anything from Jennings that afternoon, but the two seemed to enjoy each other's company during the hour we spent at the roadside compound.

Later that evening, when Michael walked onto the stage at Reynolds Auditorium, he was conspicuously channeling JHJ. The brown paper bag on his head was rolled up to about eye-level, in perfect imitation of the way Jennings wore his knit toboggan. As Pete Buck picked out the little minor-key intro to "Feeling Gravity's Pull," Michael leaned into his microphone stand. The paper bag completely hid his eyes, and the raincoat he wore contributed to a look that might be described as loony-bin hobo.

After a couple of songs Michael tossed aside the bag and removed the raincoat to reveal a drab, thrift-store dress. Eventually he took off the dress, under which he wore the baggy slacks and stretched-out t-shirt he kept on for the rest of the show. An androgynous neo-vaudeville strip-tease.

Although R.E.M. played a stellar set, they were almost upstaged by their opening act. Prior to this tour's North Carolina dates I'd been only vaguely aware of the Minutemen. There were too many new bands to keep up with, and too few that stood out. The Minutemen proved to be one of the latter—a ferocious, hardcore-punk trio who tore through a bunch of extremely short, extremely intense tunes showcasing their burly, energetic singer-guitarist D. Boon. Barking out lyrics I couldn't understand but liked the sound of, he bounced around as if spring-loaded, ending the set by leaping off the edge of the stage.

Alas, the great things foreseen for the Minutemen

were not to be. D. Boon was killed in a van wreck exactly two weeks after the Winston-Salem show and three days before Christmas. One of the sadder milestones in punk-rock history.

*

Except for the R.E.M. shows and a brief trip to Georgia for the holidays, the transitional weeks from 1985 into early '86 found me immersed in the roll-out of Ernie Mickler's *White Trash Cooking* and preparations for the next Jargon board meeting.

Ernie's book had been in the works since early in the year, with the Kentucky-based poet and bookmeister Jonathan Greene handling the design. The cover photo of a pale-skinned, frizzy-haired young woman posed with a load of watermelons was framed by a collage of packaging labels from miscellaneous recipe ingredients. The book was wire-bound for easy access, like many cookbooks, and Ernie's color photographs were nicely reproduced on coated paper, one or two to a page.

"Pretty damn cosmic!" declared publisher Jonathan Williams.

A few hundred copies arrived in Winston-Salem in mid-December. The exceedingly well-connected Philip Hanes claimed most of them, which he promptly dispatched to everyone on his Christmas list, including novelist Harper Lee, U.S. Senator William Fulbright, and actress Helen Hayes—not to mention North Carolina's leading Democratic and Republican politicians, and who knows who else.

Most of the edition went to Jargon's distributor, Inland Book Company. The other financial backers—Don, Lucinda, and a medical publisher named Kit Wolcott— each got fifty copies, and about 200 were shipped directly to me, in boxes I stacked against a wall in my increasingly cramped office.

White Trash Cooking had been rejected by multiple publishers on the basis of the title alone. The project was an orphan child looking for a home until Jargon came along. Never concerned about offending anyone, Jonathan had been publishing rarefied material for three decades, but he sensed there was something special about this one. Unique among Jargon books, it was an unabashed celebration of the common and the commonplace.

Although the *New Yorker* refused to run a paid advertisement—citing, of course, the offensive title— other periodicals and news outlets from *Vogue* to National Public Radio took favorable notice. The initial printing of 5,000 copies quickly sold out, as *White Trash Cooking* became a national phenomenon. The press attention was so favorable that mainstream publishers were suddenly interested, including several that had previously rejected Ernie's manuscript. My lone position on the Jargon front line meant that I ended up fielding the inquiries, and passing the serious ones on to Whitney and Thorns.

The Jargon Society's 1986 board meeting was held on the third weekend in January, this time at Reynolda House, the American art museum and former family home of R.J. Reynolds. Once again it was something of a circus, but this time the center ring was occupied by Ernest Matthew Mickler and his bodacious recipe book.

And a reprise of Ernie's multicolored, multilayered Grand Canyon Cake drenched in whiskey sauce, which had been such a big hit at Jonathan's birthday party. This latest version of the garish, high-octane dessert was served in heaping helpings to attendees at the Friday-night event.

Accompanying Ernie to Winston-Salem for the proceedings was the aforementioned Kit Wolcott, a dapper-looking, middle-aged gentleman with a tailored suit and a George Hamilton tan. Wolcott, whose business was publishing medical textbooks, had known Jonathan through previous connections and turned out to be responsible for introducing him to Ernie and his cookbook.

On the whole it was a much more upbeat board meeting than the first one I had organized, no doubt thanks to the smell of impending success—the aroma of down-home *White Trash Cooking*, and the money it was about to generate.

I spent a few minutes telling the board about recent developments with the Folk Art Project, including completion of the Saint EOM manuscript. I mentioned grants I aimed to submit in the spring, and my hopes of organizing one or more rock shows to benefit the project.

But the spotlight was on Ernie's book.

20. SIGNS OF THE TIMES

The newest addition to Jargon's visionary folk-art collection was the sign I'd commissioned from James Harold Jennings—"JARGON SOCIETY" rendered in wooden letters, each about six inches high, individually cut out, decoratively hand-painted, and meticulously nailed in place on a narrow, blue-painted plank. I hung it above the French doors opening into my office.

The sign exemplified the latest development in Jennings' art. He'd started enlivening some of his more easily portable works with texts in painted, cutout letters, all caps. The first pieces he made to incorporate this new feature were images of sturdy-looking women engaged in fisticuffs or wrestling matches, each hand-sawn from wood, painted in high-contrast colors, and prominently accompanied by the phrase "AMAZON FIGHT" or some variation thereon.

He brought three such pieces out from the bus and showed them to me during a solo visit I made to his place around the beginning of the year. What did I think of them, he wanted to know, and his face brightened when I blurted out my immediate, honest reaction:

"These are great! I love them!"

"I didn't know if I ought to be making things like that," he said. "I haven't shown 'em to anybody else."

"You ought to be making whatever you want to make," I told him. "You're an artist."

Jennings smiled. Then I asked him if he wanted to make a sign for the Jargon Society.

"How big you want it?" he inquired.

*

Halfway into its designated three-year run, Jargon's Southern Visionary Folk Art Project had clearly entered a new phase. My cohort Roger Manley was wrapping up negotiations toward a long-term home for Annie Hooper's houseful of biblical driftwood sculptures. Mrs. Hooper, bless her radiant soul, had died on January eleventh, and Roger had shepherded her work into the art-and-design collection of North Carolina State University in Raleigh. It was the culmination of a decade-long friendship and a dedicated preservation effort in which Jargon had been a valuable ally in the home stretch. To celebrate the university's acquisition of the work, Roger was planning a visionary folk art symposium and a big show of Hooper's art set for 1988.

I threw my energies into writing a series of new grant applications to support the project. Meanwhile I was starting to think about the visual aspect of the Saint EOM book. I was also honing in on Howard Finster, transcribing taped interviews and formulating additional questions.

I had known Howard for six years, and had informally signed on to the book project around the end of 1983. It was planned as a collaboration with California journalist and collector John Turner, who'd been amassing artworks and other visual artifacts from Finster since the late 1970s.

Living on opposite sides of the country, Turner and I hadn't met in person, and we had no written agreement, but we'd amiably conferred about the project through two years of phone calls and correspondence. My role was to provide a comprehensive text, while he was gathering and organizing visual material.

Following the same approach I'd taken with Saint EOM, I wanted to let Finster tell his own story, although there was a lot to sort out in his ongoing, stream-of-consciousness monolog. Chronology was not his strong suit. He was bad to go off on tangents—and tangents off of tangents—while never quite getting around to answering the last question you asked him.

*

Before I had a chance to visit Howard again at Paradise Garden, he came to Winston-Salem. During the second week of April the Jargon Society co-sponsored his appearance as a visiting art lecturer at Wake Forest University, where Winston-Salem's leading Finster authority was employed as the on-campus art-gallery director.

Victor Faccinto—Vict'ry, as Howard called him—was a proto-pop-surrealist painter more widely known for his provocative animated films. He'd recorded an album of Howard's singing and banjo-picking, and had exhibited Howard's work in the gallery as early as 1978. He and a group of Wake Forest students had been assisting Howard in Paradise Garden on my first-ever visit to the site, March 1980.

Our shared interest in Finster made for an easy collaboration between Victor and me. Howard gave a talk in one of the art-department lecture halls and led a day-long "workout" for students in the art building's main studio.

While he was in town, the Man of Visions encamped at Jargon President Whitney Jones' house. Married in late 1985, Whitney and our office-mate Suzanne had bought a house off of Reynolda Road. Finster spent three nights in their attic guest bedroom, whose walls were lined with white-painted wood paneling. True to his reputation for all-night creative marathons, he stayed up every night covering the wall panels with elaborate ink-marker drawings.

If he slept at all during his stay in Winston-Salem, I have no idea when it was. As usual, he seemed to be perpetually ON, reeling out his non-stop monolog, showing off his art, and delighting in the attention lavished on him. He also seemed to enjoy wearing his new, two-piece suit in a striking shade of electric Carolina blue—a perfect complement to the wide grin perpetually plastered on his face.

*

The high spirits in which Finster's visit left me were obliterated a couple of days later, when I answered the phone at my apartment. On the other end I was surprised to hear the voice of Scotty Steward, chief assistant to Eddie Martin aka EOM. He was obviously upset.

"Dude shot himself," he told me.

"Excuse me?"

"He shot himself in the head while I was at the fish place gettin' us somethin' to eat. I found him when I got back. He's gone, man."

I felt like I had been shot.

21. FAST FAREWELL

The decision to hold a graveside service the following day was made by Eddie's sister-in-law Ruth Martin, his next of kin, who lived in the nearby community of Tazewell. She clearly wanted to get this business out of the way.

Working fast, I made arrangements to be there. Jargon paid the tab. Early the next morning I flew from Greensboro to Atlanta, and then on by commuter jet to Columbus, where Scotty picked me up at the airport.

I was in Marion County, Georgia, long enough to meet a few family members gathered at Ruth's house, and to rejoin them at the outdoor service in a cemetery on the north side of Buena Vista. Scotty drove me to Pasaquan for a walk around the site before returning me to the airport. From Columbus I flew back to Atlanta, then on to Blacksburg, Virginia. I was scheduled to give a talk the following evening on a double bill with critic John Yau lecturing on Jasper Johns. It was one of several events Ray Kass had organized for his latest spring arts-extravaganza weekend. Jonathan Williams was also involved, and was there when I arrived.

Appropriately, my talk focused largely on Saint EOM and featured multiple slides of Pasaquan, including some of Jonathan's as well as others by Roger, Lucinda Bunnen, and myself. I concluded with a poem I'd written while airborne in the wake of the graveside service:

Paean for the Late Last Pasaquoyan

Yonder's that long road of sparkling sand
going off into the green trees and the blue hills
in the distance, the one you followed
as a young man out into the wide exotic unknown world

In the end it wasn't wide or exotic enough for you.

You made the world your own, remade it
in your own imaginative transformation,
your own house and garden and
head, your antennae tuned into some funky and mysterious
inner spirit world.

The flesh and food and herbal nutrients
were good enough while they lasted, interruptions
in the prevailing sense of disappointment.

You sucked this world up and spat it out
like the stuff a spider spits out
to make its web.

You rewove it in a private hypertechnicolor concrete miracle
where the past and the future came together in the present.

With that final punctuation-point projectile
BANG
you let yourself be sucked out
one tiny bloody hole among the millions

that stud the red-light-pulsing sky of history
above the jewel-encrusted highway you stepped out on
into eternity.

"There's always somethin'
over the hill,"
you said.

You, who are the wind
in the green trees
this afternoon,
scattering blossoms
over the earth.

*

"A tragic but noble act," was Jonathan's verdict on Eddie Martin's suicide. He made the remark from behind the wheel of Okra, his green Volkswagen Rabbit, following a long silence as he drove us back to North Carolina from Blacksburg that weekend.

"You doing okay?" he asked, glancing over at me in the passenger's seat. It was his way of asking whether I'd been unduly shaken by the loss.

I flashed back to my first meeting with EOM, in Jonathan's company, in the early weeks of 1980.

"Yeah, I'm okay, thanks."

It would take a few days, or weeks —maybe months— for me to absorb everything that had happened.

22. RECHARGING

In the wake of EOM's shocking exit my immediate, pragmatic concern was the book. I set about writing the new conclusion Eddie had fatally enacted, and I arranged to expand the visual components. We had already established a design concept loosely based on *The Wizard of Oz*—the 1939 film version. The volume would open in the ordinary world, as seen in black-and-white, and would brighten into full-blown color when the reader arrived at Pasaquan, the real-life equivalent of Baum's fictional Land of Oz. Guy Mendes had made black-and-white images of Buena Vista and Marion County to precede the opening texts.

As for depicting Pasaquan itself, Jonathan's color photographs were great, and we had plenty of them, but they were square-format, Rolleiflex transparencies that emphasized the site's striking, colorful details. I felt that additional images from more distanced perspectives were needed to give a sense of Eddie's overarching architectural vision.

To that end, Roger Manley and I traveled to Pasaquan in the late spring of 1986. The fate of the place remained very much up in the air. Eddie's will named two different heirs to the property—the tenuously extant county historical society, and the arts-and-sciences museum in

Columbus. Further complications stemmed from EOM's lifelong, willful neglect of his income-tax obligations.

Eddie's local attorney Wayne Jernigan retained custody of the site while these issues were being sorted out, but he sensibly allowed Fred Fussell to serve as a kind of unofficial advisor. Employed at the time as chief curator at the Columbus Museum of Arts and Sciences, Fred had known EOM for twenty years. He smoothed the way for Roger and me to visit Pasaquan unsupervised for a few days. We were allowed to sleep overnight inside the compound, and we spent most of our waking hours looking through stored artworks and related materials I'd never seen before. A trove of news clippings, vintage photos, and other papers turned up in the attic, along with carefully sealed boxes of drawings, sketchbooks, and paintings. I selected a number of the photos for reproduction in the book.

Key to our plans for the trip was a panoramic camera Roger had recently acquired. He used it to make several 180-degree exterior views, and he extensively documented the interior with color-slide film using a 35-millimeter camera.

*

While we were in Georgia, Roger and I also visited Paradise Garden, whose dense, maze-like layout rendered it especially challenging to visually capture in a panoramic format. Roger managed to turn this feature of the environment to his advantage in compositions that downplay the claustrophobia in the interest of specific details.

Roger was seeing Howard's place for the second time, but he'd been rushed during his first visit, so he was glad to have a couple of days to take it all in. We spent the nights in the steadily progressing World's Folk Art Church, where Howard had fixed up a couple of guest rooms. These were in the original, one-story building he was still in the process of augmenting with a tiered, multi-story tower up top—a project "blueprinted by God," as he put it. Roger made photographs of the garden, the church, and much of the art that was on display pretty much everywhere, while I spent most of my time following Howard around and interviewing him in the small, art-glutted house he used as a studio. Even the asbestos panels of the front room's ceiling were covered with drawings. The latter were made by some of Howard's appreciative visitors—those nimble enough to stand on a chair while drawing on the ceiling.

In some ways Howard was the easiest subject I'd ever interviewed, but he was such a prodigious talker it was always hard to find an opening for a question. When I did manage to interject a few words, he often launched into a tangential story without ever addressing the point I'd raised. He was also fond of re-telling stories I'd already heard multiple times. He loved hearing himself talk, and he probably kept the monolog going even when no one else was around.

My usual practice was to tape-record these sessions while simultaneously making copious notes. I learned to stop writing—and sometimes switch off the recorder—when Howard segued into auto-pilot mode and started re-playing familiar anecdotes and listing the formidable accomplishments he'd already told me about countless times.

A natural multi-tasker, he often painted while we talked, and the television in his studio was almost always on with the sound usually muted. Seated in front of his easel, he leaned in to focus on the fine brushwork of his meandering textual passages and tiny images of flying angels, heavenly mansions, and happy-face clouds while the words poured out of him. He typically kept at it into the wee hours, and I never once heard him say he was tired and needed rest. On more than one occasion after we'd been at it all night, I stumbled into the adjoining room, lay down on a cot wedged against the front wall, and fell asleep to the sound of Howard's voice.

Where did he get all the energy?

He drank lots of coffee and ate lots of sweets. Sometimes he ate instant coffee by the spoonful after stirring in a little hot water and sugar. But the combined effects of these fuels didn't fully account for it. There was another aspect to his seemingly ceaseless talk and activity. A clinician might peg it as mania, but I attributed it to what William Blake identified as "eternal delight."

*

One morning while Howard was entertaining a busload of visiting art collectors and curiosity seekers, Roger and I went for a little ride in order to follow up some information passed on to us by Jeff Gilley, my attorney friend in Athens, who grew up in Summerville. Howard's nephew Allen Wilson confirmed the details and gave us more precise driving directions.

Thus did we find ourselves at the isolated rural compound of James B. Lemming, alongside a blacktop county road south of Trion, Georgia. We knew it was the right place because it was a small, tumbledown farmhouse covered with handmade targets and other geometric forms along with carefully placed, ordinary objects, all painted in combinations of red, blue, white, and black.

The house was set back from the road at least 100 yards, and there was no lawn to speak of— just a surrounding expanse of weed-pocked white dirt and red clay, with scrawny pines and dwarf oak trees growing here and there. Most of the visible landscape had been clearcut in recent years. The trunks of a few remaining pines near the house were painted fire-engine red, and several were embellished with plastic gallon milk jugs, paint-can lids, and other objects nailed into the bark.

Roger steered his van into the narrow dirt driveway and followed it to a small clearing near the house. As we exited the vehicle we were greeted by a short, stocky, white-haired man who wandered out of the front door and stood on the rickety, target-cluttered porch looking down at us.

"How y'all doin'?" he inquired.

Fine, thanks, we said. "You must be Mister Lemming."

"Yeah. James B. Lemming, that's me. Who are y'all?"

Wearing a white t-shirt, a filthy baseball cap, blue denim overalls, and loosely laced, paint-spattered work boots, he looked rumpled and half asleep. He was slowly masticating a hunk of tobacco. After a minute he spat some brown juice into the dirt beyond the porch.

We introduced ourselves, complimented him on his yard decor, and asked if we could take some pictures of the place. He watched us photograph his home's exterior and yard—obviously a source of pride—then he invited us indoors.

The interior was a mess and appeared to have been partly demolished. A wall between the living room and kitchen had been knocked out, leaving the rough edges of plaster and old wood visible and potentially hazardous. A couple of worn-looking stuffed chairs and an end table furnished the living room, enlivened by a few conspicuous decorative touches. The bricks around the fireplace had been painted red, white, and blue in a symmetrical pattern, and a pair of idiosyncratically altered landscape paintings hung on the soot-blackened wall above the mantel.

They looked like pieces of vintage generic motel art—bland vistas showing trees on hilly lakesides. Each painting had been augmented with a single red disk painted dead-center, with a white plastic fast-food fork horizontally clamped or glued across it.

The plastic forks visually cued me to notice their counterparts on the end table—two ordinary metal-flatware table forks, side by side. I also caught sight of the nearby wall outlet, into one socket of which was a standard plug whose black-insulated electrical cord had been chopped off and disconnected from whatever electronic appliance it had originally belonged to.

The cord's two wires were pulled apart with the insulation stripped away to expose about an inch of the hairlike copper strands on either side. It was loosely stretched up at an angle from the outlet and draped over a nail in the wall four or five feet above the floor, so the live current was readily available.

We'd been told about this routine, but of course we wanted to see it for ourselves.

"What's going on here, Mr. Lemming?" I inquired,

gesturing toward the bare wires at the end of the plugged-in cord.

He shifted the wad of tobacco in his jaw and said, "That's how I charge myself up. Look here, I'll show you."

He dusted his hands with corn starch from a plastic container alongside the metal forks, which he then picked up, one in each hand.

"Helps me get a better connection," he explained. Then he turned to face the wall and used his thumbs to push the fork tines onto the bare wires, thereby completing the circuit with his own body. He began to vibrate almost imperceptibly, then more vigorously as he glanced over his shoulder at me and kept talking. A tiny stream of tobacco juice drooled from one corner of his mouth.

"See there?" he said. "I can feel that energy flowing right up one arm and out the other. Charging me right up!"

Neither his inscrutable face nor his flat tone of voice changed during this startling performance. After about thirty seconds he disconnected himself and placed the forks back on the table, then he shuffled across the room to an alcove I suddenly realized was his exercise studio. His face was beet-red, and he was sweating and breathing more audibly, still chewing on that plug of tobacco.

"It makes you stouter and ever'thing," he said by way of explanation. I gathered that he administered his self-electrocution regimen multiple times every day. And "stout" was apparently his word for "strong."

To demonstrate this surge of charged-up physical strength he hoisted a couple of home-made lifting weights, each consisting of a metal chain attached to a cinderblock. He lifted them several times, extending his elbows out to the sides like fledgling bird wings. Then he started bare-fist hitting a regulation punching bag suspended from the ceiling.

Following this demonstration he led us outside, down the front steps, and out to the far end of his driveway, where an ancient-looking pickup truck was parked with the hood raised. He showed us how he could use the truck battery for the same purpose by connecting opposite hands to the battery poles using customized jumper-cable clamps.

The truck didn't look like it had been driven in a long time.

I would later learn that James B. Lemming had once maintained an active career as a moonshine-runner—a real-life version of Robert Mitchum's *Thunder Road* character. During a late-night delivery he had a near-fatal wreck while trying to outrun the law. He was released from the hospital after an extended stay, but he'd never been right since then, according to family members.

He was convinced the doctors who'd saved his life had turned his eyeballs around backwards.

23. MATRIARCH

DeWitt Chatham Hanes was Philip's widowed mother, well into her eighties by the time I met her in 1985. She inhabited and presided over the family estate from a big, red-brick, Georgian-Revival house with slender white columns, right across the pond from SECCA's backyard.

A bundle of contradictions was DeWitt Hanes, who had partied with Scott and Zelda Fitzgerald during the Roaring Twenties and lately sent regular donations to Jim and Tammy Baker's PTL Club.

The occasion of our first meeting was unforgettable, in part because it also marked my first meeting with Maya Angelou, among the few guests the Hanes family matriarch had invited to an informal gathering at her house that afternoon. Also present were Tom Meyer, Jonathan Williams, and another tall, balding gentleman whose name was Jim Moon—artist, art teacher, arts patron, and pillar of the North Carolina Piedmont's gay community. He and Jonathan were of the same generation, and they seemed to already know each other, although perhaps not closely.

Maya Angelou was still new in Winston-Salem, where she had bought a home in 1982, when Wake Forest University awarded her a professorship in American Studies. Doctor Angelou, as she insisted on being addressed by all but her closest friends. I was struck by her distinctively deep, unplaceably accented voice and her broad, straight-mouthed smile.

We were an odd assortment of characters, sizing each other up and not knowing quite what to say—or at least such was the case with me. After introductions all around, Jonathan exchanged a few pleasantries with our hostess, and everyone fell silent for a moment while DeWitt gazed around the room, smiling like the cat that ate the canary.

I wanted to tell Doctor Angelou how much I appreciated her book *I Know Why the Caged Bird Sings*, but I'd never done more than skim a bookstore copy, and I couldn't think of anything else of hers I might have read, so I kept my mouth shut.

"I have a surprise for you," DeWitt announced, then she clapped her hands twice, and five middle-aged, African American women in crisp white uniforms filed into the cozy sitting room. These were DeWitt's house servants, most of whom I had met a few minutes earlier, on my arrival with Jonathan and Tom through a side door from the driveway into the spacious kitchen.

"Come out and sing one for us!" DeWitt instructed them, beaming happily. "Y'all are going to love this!" she promised us.

Whereupon her five employees arrayed themselves in front of the doorway to the dining room, facing us as they struck up an a cappella gospel tune worthy of the Staples Singers. It was a truly impressive vocal feat with pitch-perfect close harmonies. But the scenario was uncomfortably reminiscent of a command performance down on de old plantation.

I glanced across the room at Doctor Angelou, sitting back in a stuffed armchair with her ankles crossed and both hands resting atop the elegant, polished-wood cane vertically poised in front of her. She cocked her head, listening expressionlessly.

DeWitt was one of those "Great Southern Ladies," to borrow Jonathan's term. Pale-skinned, white-haired, and diminutive, she was on that day casually attired in gray wool slacks, a festive red sweater, and sparkly gold bedroom slippers. She reminded me of my maternal grandmother and her contemporaries in Mississippi. I had always gotten along splendidly with women of that class and age.

*

Following this initial meeting, DeWitt took to calling me on the phone every few weeks. Taking a special interest in Jargon's Folk Art Project, she began collecting pieces by some of the artists we were documenting, and eventually selling some of them from a mountain crafts shop she operated with her daughter in Roaring Gap, an affluent resort community in the mountains north of Winston-Salem.

Her distinctively hoarse, tobacco-cured patrician drawl was immediately recognizable whenever she phoned me.

"Hello, Tom, this is DeWitt," she would greet me. "Next time you go down to Georgia to see that Reverend Finster I want you to bring me back some of those funny little pieces he makes with the writing all over them."

She was especially fond of Finster's miniature cutout portraits of himself brandishing a Bible and standing on a wooden plank covered with free-form sermonizing in his urgent, creatively spelled, upper-case script. He made them in multiples and sold them inexpensively as souvenirs—his own term for them. He distinguished them from each other by altering the colors of his suit, which he sometimes covered with happy-face clouds, and writing a fresh text for each unpainted plank base.

I must have brought DeWitt at least four of these pieces over a couple of years, along with other Finster multiples including cheetah cats, trumpeting angels, baby Elvises, and variations on a dinosaur-like critter he called an *Abigrilla*. I also helped her acquire pieces by Georgia Blizzard and James Harold Jennings, most of which went on sale at her shop.

When I delivered these items to Hanes Manor, DeWitt always invited me in for a drink or coffee and a visit in the familiar downstairs sitting room. A lifelong smoker, like almost everyone else in Winston-Salem, she employed a refined mode of extinguishing a finished cigarette. In lieu of ashtrays, gilt-ringed porcelain saucers were strategically placed in the sitting room for her and her guests. Each saucer held a small, gold cylinder open at one end, somewhat resembling a bullet's shell-casing but thicker, like a thimble, and shinier. The idea was to insert the glowing butt end of the spent cigarette into this golden bauble, leaving it resting on the saucer, to be whisked away by servants.

Sometimes DeWitt told stories of her youthful adventures with the Lost Generation, during the early years of her marriage to her beloved Ralph (1898-1973). Once, she told me, he had driven the two of them across the Mojave Desert with huge bags of ice strapped to the hood of their roadster and the convertible windshield opened to the ice-cooled breeze—an early, unofficial prototype for the automobile air-conditioner, jerry-rigged by a clever textile-company heir fifteen years before the first mass-produced versions.

By the time I met DeWitt she lived luxuriously alone and apparently spent several hours each day watching television. A devout Christian—Methodist, I think— she was an avid follower of the PTL (Praise the Lord) Club, Jim and Tammy Bakker's TV show and related evangelically themed enterprises. An ideal devotee, from the Bakkers' standpoint—loyal, attentive, and generous with the substantial largesse she had at her disposal. No telling how much money she had sent to their massive non-profit enterprise.

DeWitt could be counted on to give Jargon a few hundred dollars a year, but frankly I don't think she was much interested in the poetry and photography books Jonathan published. Our Folk Art Project was another matter, though, since it dovetailed with her interest in Appalachian crafts.

*

One day in the spring of 1986 DeWitt phoned me with a surprise request.

"Today is my wedding anniversary," she informed me. "Ralph's been gone for thirteen years, and I miss him every day, but I'm in the mood to celebrate, and I don't want to see anyone in my family. I want you to take me out for a date!"

She couldn't see my startled expression. I paused only for a moment before assuring her I would be honored to escort her.

"I don't want to go anywhere fancy, just someplace fun, so how about the Rose and Thistle?"

"That's fine with me," I told her. "Diana's working there tonight, and I know she'll be glad to see you."

The popular restaurant and sometimes music-venue was just a few blocks from our house. Diana had recently joined the wait staff, which also provided part-time employment to several other local artists. I had introduced her to DeWitt a few months earlier, and the two of them had hit it off.

"Oh, good!" DeWitt exclaimed, then she added, "I hope she won't be jealous!"

"Yes, I hope not!"

DeWitt roared laughing.

"What time shall I pick you up?"

"How about seven o'clock."

"I'll see you at seven, then."

DeWitt was adorable that evening in a lavender, cotton pullover sweater and little matching bows in her hair. We sat opposite each other in one of the booths alongside the front counter, and received special attention from Diana and other servers. Owner Mike Turko stopped by our table to say hello, and I introduced him to my date for the evening.

"You know I've always been attracted to older women, Mike," I stage-whispered behind my left hand.

I probably met a dozen members of the Hanes family during my first couple of years in Winston-Salem, and I would meet a few more of them in the years that followed.

DeWitt was my favorite.

24. IN THE WORKS

Far-reaching changes were brewing in Winston-Salem's business community during my first year on the Jargon payroll. In 1985 the locally beloved, fabulously profitable R.J. Reynolds—increasingly viewed by the broader public as an evil purveyor of cancer-sticks—merged with Nabisco, a name brand popularly associated with vanilla wafers and other wholesome snack products. Nabisco's top dog Ross Johnson, who became RJR Nabisco's president and chief operating officer, moved to town about a year after I did. In the fall of 1986 this large-living Canadian high-roller was promoted to CEO, and within the year he would become vilified in local circles for relocating the corporate headquarters to—of all places—Atlanta, my former hometown.

Winston-Salem, where the Reynolds Tobacco company had been founded more than a century earlier, was too "bucolic" for Johnson.

But that's getting ahead of my story, and off our cultural track.

In the rarefied universe of the Jargon Society, as of 1986, most of the attention was on *White Trash Cooking*. The first printing of Ernie Mickler's sassy little culinary blockbuster—5,000 copies—sold out within weeks, so we printed more. By the middle of the year there were

25,000 copies in print. The book was reviewed in *People* magazine, the *New York Times*, the *Village Voice*, and the *Weekly World News*, among other mags and rags.

At the home office in Winston-Salem, I became a de-facto mail-order clerk, working overtime to fill individual orders for the book, which had quickly become too big for Jargon to handle. In late June Whitney and Thorns flew to New York to meet with several big-time publishers vying to buy the rights. All offered sums in the mid-five-figure range and—by the way—insisted on retaining the rights to make changes.

No dice, JW decreed.

Cheeky of Jargon to turn down such sums. Ernie Mickler, who'd never had much money, certainly thought so. For Jonathan it was simply a matter of principle, but it seemed to work as a kind of non-intentional business strategy. The offers kept coming in, soon ratcheting up into the six-figure range.

The winning bidder turned out to be Ten Speed Press, a West Coast outfit whose publisher Phil Wood was something of a maverick like Jonathan. Their breakout best-seller was the *Moosewood Cookbook*, so they appeared to be a natural choice to take on Ernie's book. Wood and his associates sent Jargon a clever, photo-illustrated package promoting their offer's advantages, not the least of which were financial. They proposed to pay more than any other publisher, including a higher royalty fee, and they promised no changes to the original except for a title-page revision to include Ten Speed's name alongside the Jargon Society's.

Once the deal was sealed they moved fast, printing 160,000 copies by mid-November. Their accountants projected net profits of $100,000 before Christmas. To celebrate, Ten Speed invited Jargon to hold our January 1987 board meeting in its hometown, Berkeley. In the fall we began planning the occasion, and it fell to me to make most of the arrangements.

*

Amid all the hoopla for Ernie's book, I was striving mightily to keep the Folk Art Project from being forgotten. Still outstripping its budget going into its final year, it was being funded largely with *White Trash Cooking* profits.

In the summer of '86 I completed three new chapters to insert at the end of the EOM book, accounting for Eddie's suicide and its aftermath. All photos for the book were selected and sequenced, and *New York Times* art critic John Russell—a longtime friend of JW—agreed to write an introduction. Jonathan's *Big Book of Southern Folk Art* was still in the works, as was the Finster book.

One of the losing bidders in the White Trash publishers' sweepstakes was Random House, where there was also some interest in our folk-art books. Well aware of Finster's rising-star status in the art world, their acquisitions people were especially intrigued by the prospect of a book about him. Late that summer they dispatched Jeff Stone, an up-and-coming editor and publishing associate, to meet with us in Winston-Salem. I took him to see Richard Craven's big "Contemporary Southeastern Folk Art" exhibit, which had recently opened at SECCA, and out to meet James Harold Jennings at the latter's roadside "art world" near Pilot Mountain.

Jeff talked with me about the possibility of publishing the EOM and Finster books under Random House's Knopf or Vintage imprints. Back in New York, he and his colleague David Rosenthal followed up with phone calls to both Jonathan and John Turner.

There were other signs the larger culture was starting to catch up with us. An article on Kentucky gourd-sculptor Minnie Black—a favorite of Jonathan—appeared in *ARTnews* that summer, and the *Wall Street Journal* ran a front-page feature piece about Finster. Meanwhile, some of my fundraising efforts finally began to pay off. The Southern Arts Federation awarded $7,500 to support a traveling Saint EOM retrospective I was to co-curate with Fred Fussell, and the Lyndhurst Foundation gave the Folk Art Project two grand, which we would apply toward the EOM book.

Mindful of the Folk Art Project's original time frame,

I was thinking it merited an extension. Almost halfway into the third year there was still much to be done.

*

In the meantime, tragedy struck. Toward summer's end, Kit Wolcott— the medical publisher who introduced us to Ernie Mickler and helped bankroll his book—died of AIDS. A shocking, sudden loss.

Our immediate concern, of course, was that Ernie might be at risk.

25. VISIONARY MISSIONARY

The interval from late '86 into early '87 found me often out of the office traveling. In October I went to Bethlehem, Pennsylvania, to give a slide talk on Howard Finster at Lehigh University. The on-campus art gallery's director Ricardo Viera and a religion professor named Norman Girardot—both Finster enthusiasts—had co-curated a "Finster Family Exhibition" featuring works by Finster, his daughter Beverly, grandson Michael, and nephew Allen Wilson, all of whom had taken up art-making.

I had developed an introduction to Finster and his art that aimed to evoke the experience of visiting Paradise Garden and meeting the self-proclaimed Man of Visions—an abbreviated version of what I wanted to do with the book. The text consisted entirely of Finster's own words as I'd transcribed and edited them from my notes and recordings, delivered in my best approximation of his voice, with its southern-Appalachian twang and evangelical preacher's cadence.

While talking more or less non-stop, à la Finster, I used a remote control device to advance the projected slides of his work, including individual pieces and views of his garden environment, sometimes with him in the frame, and sometimes showing parts of his free-form church tower in progress. It was a mix of images by Roger, Jonathan, Victor Faccinto, myself, and others, presented one-by-one, at a fairly rapid pace, and without explanation. I was going for a dizzying effect that I judged appropriate to the subject.

I arrived at Lehigh only a few weeks after an appearance by Finster himself, so my audience had already been primed. The multi-generational Finster residency worked well as a set-up for my presentation, with its emphasis on Paradise Garden, which the students of course had not seen.

Gallery director Viera, on the other hand, had visited Finster's garden several times in the company of his faculty collaborator. Atlanta native Norman Girardot's academic specialty was Taoism, or Daoism, as he rendered it. He viewed Finster as a latter-day Daoist sage transposed to the American Deep South. Norman was my host during my three days on and around the Lehigh campus—the start of an enduring, collegial friendship.

From Pennsylvania I returned by way of New York to North Carolina, whereupon I drove across the state to Rocky Mount. Among its other distinctions Rocky Mount was the home of North Carolina Wesleyan College, where I'd been booked to give a reading. My host in this case was English professor Leverett T. Smith, aka Terry, whom I'd known for years. He was a connoisseur of contemporary literature and art, and we shared an enthusiasm for the Black Mountain writers.

As a visiting writer at N.C. Wesleyan I joined the distinguished company of Joel Oppenheimer, Fielding Dawson, Paul Metcalf, Michael Rumaker, and of course Jonathan Williams, all of whom Terry hosted at one time or another during the years the college was lucky enough to have him on the faculty. These readings and residencies were typically accompanied by a commissioned chapbook or broadsheet published under the NCWC imprint.

When Terry asked me for something along these lines I sent him the poem I'd written to memorialize Saint EOM after the graveside ceremony six months earlier in Georgia. The broadsheet poem was printed on yellow card stock alongside a reproduction of a vintage sketchbook page on which EOM had long ago drawn handsome, androgynous figures with long, upswept hair. Copies were passed out to the audience at my reading, which incorporated slide projections of the Pasaquan compound. I was given a stack of them along with my modest fee of two-hundred dollars and expenses.

*

Meanwhile, the book I'd worked on for three years with Eddie Owens Martin was finally headed for publication—a bittersweet milestone, since its subject wouldn't be around to see it. To design *St. EOM in the*

Land of Pasaquan, Jonathan chose his contemporary Joyce Kachergis, whom he'd initially known as the design-and-production manager for the University of North Carolina Press. More recently she'd established her own company operating out of her home in the woods south of Chapel Hill—a secluded site that I visited with increasing frequency toward the end of the year, while Jonathan and Tom were in England.

I liked Joyce. She immediately 'got' our *Wizard of Oz*-inspired concept, and she loved Eddie's story. She dove into the project and soon had impressive results to show. When she discovered the Atlantis typeface and tried it out for the display type—the main title and chapter titles—she laughed out loud, she told me. It was so outrageously baroque, not unlike the molten-looking texts on psychedelic rock-concert posters. It was perfect, she thought, and I agreed. Perfect.

*

In early November Roger Manley and I revisited the Light Factory in Charlotte, where we gave back-to-back slide presentations about some of the art we'd been documenting. Later that month I went to Atlanta for a meeting of the American Academy of Religion, ostensibly to serve on a panel concerning visionary art.

Mid-December found me back in Winston-Salem for yet another meeting with New York publishing reps. Jeff

Stone again, this time accompanied by David Rosenthal, on behalf of Random House subsidiary Vintage Books. Jonathan, Whitney, Thorns, and I sat down with the two of them to discuss a potential joint publication deal for the EOM, Finster, and JW folk-art books. They brought a passel of merchandise promoting Vintage's new book about Max Headroom, the computer-generated personality at the center of an eponymous TV show. I wondered to myself if they foresaw a similar merchandising blitz for the Finster book.

Once again the talks sparked short-term optimism but didn't yield any immediate action, leaving me glad Jargon was moving on the EOM book without any collaborative baggage.

After the usual December holidays I put it all on the mental back burner so I could give full attention to the impending Jargon board meeting and related activities in Berkeley and San Francisco.

26. BAGHDAD BY THE BAY

Halfway into my thirties, and I'd never been to California—hard to believe, but true. It seemed fitting that my first West Coast trip would be a cultural mission.

I was charged with making arrangements for Jargon board members and special guests flying in from various parts of the country. The assignment occupied much of my time in the first weeks of the New Year. Our Bay-Area headquarters was to be the Claremont Hotel, a sprawling, well-appointed resort in the wooded hills overlooking Berkeley. In addition to guest rooms I booked meeting rooms, made catering arrangements, and coordinated with Ernie Mickler about yet another of his now-famous Grand Canyon Cakes.

Jonathan had longstanding connections in the Bay Area, a nexus of post-war American poetry and gay culture. He pulled some of those strings to arrange a Jargon event at the San Francisco Art Institute.

In advance of our appointments out west I'd contacted John Turner, who lived in Berkeley. I let him know about our plans and inquired about getting together with him. Evidently eager to meet me face-to-face, he insisted I stay at his house instead of the Claremont. After landing at San Francisco International Airport I took a cab to his cozy bungalow, whose tiny front yard was jammed with flowering plants and shrubs.

John struck me as a likable guy, generally confirming my impression from three years of sporadic correspondence and phone conversations. He'd studied at the California College of Arts and Crafts in Oakland, worked as a cultural correspondent for a Bay-Area television station, and traveled widely, with a clear preference for exotic locales. A few years my senior, he was dark-eyed with a fringe of black hair around the sides and back of his gleaming bald head. He wore wire-rimmed eyeglasses and casual conservative clothing—nothing extravagant or overtly pretentious about him. His demeanor was intense, though, and he was sharply focused on our project. Sensing some impatience, I updated him on my efforts vis-a-vis Finster. I was likewise curious to assess the progress he'd made in selecting and organizing visual material.

The interior of John's house was a testament to his travels and collecting habits—comfortable if tightly configured, the walls and shelves densely arrayed with photographs, trade signs, art, and lots of carved coconut heads. Even the bathroom was filled with art and idiosyncratic artifacts. Not surprisingly, there were dozens of paintings and other works by Howard Finster, with Turner himself portrayed in several of them.

*

A whirlwind of activities occupied me during my West Coast week. The board meeting came off smoothly, if somewhat awkwardly for me. In my report for the group I summarized the status of the Saint EOM book and the Folk Art Project, scheduled to conclude in only five months. To encourage an extension into a fourth year, I emphasized our progress, fundraising successes, co-publishing negotiations, and my ongoing efforts to arrange benefit concerts by some of my musician friends.

Alas, I got the impression some of the assembled Jargonauts were tired of hearing about it. The extension didn't seem likely. Jargon's decision-makers clearly had other financial priorities. I was slow to realize the obvious—that their primary goal was to secure Jonathan's future, to the extent possible. Jargon's archive, which JW had compiled over more than thirty-five years, had recently been acquired by SUNY-Buffalo's special-collections library. The deal was structured around a convoluted investment arrangement designed to yield a modest monthly income. Details were still being ironed out.

Meanwhile, the windfall profits from Ernie's book could theoretically be used to bankroll future Jargon publications, but they also carried the potential to seed a modest endowment—a goal to which longtime board members understandably aspired.

The hashing out of Jargon business was interrupted by other activities, scheduled and unscheduled. At the top of the bill was the Saturday-afternoon Jargon extravaganza on an auditorium stage at the San Francisco Art Institute. JW gave one of his inspired readings, as did Bay Area poet and Jargon author James Broughton; Roger Manley treated attendees to one of his epic slide talks; and I channeled Saint EOM while projecting slides of Pasaquan. The auditorium was packed, and the audience was demonstrably appreciative.

Other Bay Area residents I saw while out there included Jonathan's lifelong friend Gene Ramey, an art consultant whose apartment we visited; filmmaker Dana Atchley, who'd shot many hours of footage of Saint EOM at Pasaquan; and poet Ronald Johnson, author of several Jargon titles, and Jonathan's significant other in the pre-Tom Meyer era. Roger Manley and I both remained on the West Coast for a few days after the board meeting, allowing visits to City Lights Bookstore, Golden Gate Park, the Haight-Ashbury district, and other points of interest.

The layover also enabled me to spend more time with my host. I got a brief look at John Turner's impressive trove of Finster ephemera, which filled a walk-in closet in his home. There were faded snapshots of Finster's early outdoor artworks, handwritten notecards, clippings of

Finster's old columns for his local newspaper, and prints Finster had produced on a crude lithography press, often centering on a mug-shot photo from the 1940s. There was enough great material to fill several books.

John drove us all over the Bay Area, allowing us to cruise some outdoor art sites and other points of interest while we talked. He did most of the talking, and much of the time he seemed to be thinking aloud.

Again, I found him generally amiable, and was impressed with the Finster material he'd assembled. He certainly hadn't oversold it to me. It was a formidable archive, although I couldn't see that he had done much to organize it for our purposes.

In any case, for a few days the prospects for our fruitful collaboration toward a definitive Finster book seemed assured.

But then John Turner turned on me. Literally overnight.

On my second-to-last morning in Berkeley, I woke up and dressed, got some coffee, and joined John in his living room.

I think his exact words were, "You're off the book."

"Excuse me?" I said, blowing steam off my coffee.

"I don't want you involved in the Howard book. I'm going to do it myself."

Returning John's gaze with raised eyebrows, I reminded him I'd been working on this book for three years.

The exchange continued in this vein for a couple of minutes before the clear moment when I suddenly understood the dynamic. John Turner felt he'd originated a project that had slipped from his grasp. Furthermore, he'd been upset by my reading from the EOM book, and by the entire Jargon event at the Art Institute.

The program's more boldly homophilic aspects—some of Jonathan's poetry, much of James Broughton's reading, and Eddie Martin's account of his hustling days in New York—had rubbed John Turner very much the wrong way, he let me know. If he didn't use the word 'unwholesome' he certainly implied it by way of informing me he didn't want to be associated with any such business. And he was certain Howard Finster would feel likewise.

John Turner was clearly unaware of Finster's longstanding friendship with Eddie Martin, and his broad-minded views about sexuality and gender preferences. But never mind. I could tell it would be pointless to argue.

Timing probably played a part in John's startling turnabout. It was the peak of the AIDS crisis, when untold numbers of gay men were sick and dying in and around San Francisco. Homophobia was resurgent, even in this region long known for its live-and-let-live attitude toward personal behavior. I was unaware of John's sexual leanings, whatever they might have been, but our suddenly tense exchange yielded all the clarification I needed.

In any case, whatever John decided to do with his archives, I was still working on a book about Howard Finster. I had most of what was needed toward a coherent, comprehensive narrative, and ready access to plenty of photographs and other visuals, not to mention a publisher—and the ongoing talks with Jeff Stone, David Rosenthal et al, which I felt might yield a higher-profile deal for the book.

I also knew I'd brought John Turner in on those talks, and he would pursue his own discussions with the New York people. He told me as much.

27. GEARING UP AND WINDING DOWN

A lmost immediately after returning from the West Coast I threw myself into an effort we'd been planning for a few months—relocating Jargon headquarters. The new digs was a freestanding, one-story modernist building on Brookstown Avenue, directly behind the repurposed Tudor house where I'd worked for more than two years. I recruited a couple of assistants to help me move the bookshelves, tables, electric typewriter, visionary folk-art collection, and boxes of books across the driveway.

Originally an architect's office, the flat-roofed structure was sheathed in dark-stained wood, and its entrance was oriented to the middle of the block with a red-brick walkway leading around from a street-side parking area for three or four cars. The courtyard door opened onto the largest room, opposite a built-in desk extending just below a row of louvered, single-pane windows overlooking the street.

In addition to the large room where I set up my work station and displayed much of the Jargon folk-art collection, the wood-paneled interior also included a narrow hallway that accessed a full bathroom with a shower stall and smaller offices or multi-purpose rooms, two of which I used mostly for storage. The rent was twice what we'd paid for our one-room office with kitchen access, but thanks to Ernie Mickler and Ten Speed Press, Jargon could afford it.

I suppose the new headquarters encouraged me to think there might still be a chance for extending our Folk Art Project, which had taken on a life of its own. We were starting to be noticed by people who'd never previously heard of the Jargon Society. The High Museum of Art in Atlanta booked me to give a slide lecture on the project in late February, as did the Marietta-Cobb Fine Arts Center, in Atlanta's northwest suburbs.

Among the attendees at the latter event were two individuals soon to emerge as major figures on the southern folk-art scene—Judith McWillie and William Arnett, who approached me immediately after my talk and introduced themselves. They were working together on a curatorial project that would eventually yield a landmark exhibition of African American vernacular art and several groundbreaking books. Although I hadn't previously met either of them, I knew who they were.

Judy was an art professor at the University of Georgia in Athens, a colleague of my friends Andy Nasisse and Jim Herbert. Until then I'd been unaware of her expertise on southern black vernacular art. Bill was an Atlanta art dealer and collector known for his interest in and knowledgeability about traditional arts of Africa and Asia. I was interested—and pleased—to find him expanding into American visionary art. During our brief conversation outside the arts center I exchanged contact information with them and briefly discussed our thematically overlapping projects.

While in Georgia I spent a couple of days with Howard Finster, attempting to tie up loose ends in the narrative component of our book. As usual, it was hard to steer his focus toward biographical details I wanted to clarify, but I was able to get at least some of what I came for, and I enjoyed the time with him.

In fact, Howard's time was becoming conspicuously limited. His exploding popularity came with increasing demands for his attention from visiting journalists, art scholars, indy-rock pilgrims, art tourists, and collectors phoning from far afield to reserve his latest paintings in progress, sight unseen.

*

It took a couple of months to get everything situated and presentable-looking in Jargon's new, expanded headquarters. We held an invitational opening at the beginning of spring. It seemed portentous that it was April Fools Day and snowing. The weather didn't keep folks away, though, and the event was covered in the local and regional press. *White Trash Cooking* had put Jargon on the map.

Meanwhile, on the other side of the country, my

erstwhile collaborator John Turner was speedily—and frantically, I imagined—pursuing his own talks with the New York publishing reps. Before the year was half over, Alfred Knopf, a Random House division, would announce its forthcoming publication of Turner's book *Howard Finster: Man of Visions*—still unwritten, I was sure.

Not that I'd finished my own Finster book, but at least I had most of the material I needed in the form of neatly typed transcripts of my taped interviews with Howard. I began annotating photocopies I made of these scripts, then I cut them up with scissors and re-arranged them, aiming to create a chronological narrative in Finster's own voice, as it were.

My Jargon Society associates were well aware of John Turner's shenanigans, which were successful as far as they went. And of course the Jargonauts had been in the loop on plans for my Finster book.

Imagine my surprise, then, when Jonathan did an abrupt about-face regarding Finster.

To recap: My involvement in writing about Finster had been Jonathan's idea, hatched during his initial phone conversation with John Turner back in December of 1983. All stemming from Finster's mention of Turner's idea for a book, just a few months after Jonathan had committed to publish my book about Saint EOM.

Jonathan's exact words to me at the time: "How would

you like to write a book about the Reverend Finster, too?"

My ready agreement to his proposal set off the whole chain of developments leading up to that moment, including the appointment to my nebulously administrative professional post and my relocation from Atlanta. I had been working on and talking up the Finster book for three years, all based on a gentlemen's agreement with Jonathan. On which he was suddenly reneging!

Here's how he put it in an epistle typed to me on July fifteenth: "The more I have seen of the Rev. Howard the more trouble I have had in swallowing the folk-art-dealer hardline that we are in the presence of a great artistic and spiritual figure. I smell snake oil, etc." Describing Howard as a "curious old crock of shit and sublimity," he concluded: "The idea of publishing a book about him leaves me cold."

Not lost on me was the irony that it was the third anniversary of my move to Winston-Salem.

Before firing off the angry reply I felt like writing, I thought the matter over in light of what I knew about Jonathan's idiosyncratic elitism. He was understandably reluctant to endorse a fundamentalist Christian, to the extent Howard was one. And Howard had probably just become too popular for Jonathan's liking. He no longer qualified among the creative outcasts JW had made a habit of publishing. He'd been cast from the outside in. Way in!

Still, I felt like I'd been left holding the bag of cancelled promises.

Developments with the Saint EOM book were more encouraging. Even though Jargon had bankrolled most of my field research, I was issued a $5,000 advance on royalties. It seemed rather like a consolation prize for being cut loose on the Finster book, and for the Folk Art Project's expiration. The Jargon board had nixed my suggestion to extend it beyond the original three-year run, so it was officially over as of July 1. I wasn't happy about it, but of course I knew that expenses had consistently outstripped funding for the project.

28. SYNERGETICS

Although the Jargon Society maintained no public profile, local press coverage of events like our exhibition and word-of-mouth accounts of our projects generated a measure of public curiosity. As a result, kindred or even not-so-kindred spirits sometimes phoned the office to learn more or made their way to my door to see for themselves what we were up to. I tried to remain open and prepared for such interruptions, and ever-willing to explain Jargon's "mission" or discuss the art we had on display.

One day in early 1987, soon after I'd settled into the new, more spacious office, I was attending to some business at my desk. It was mid-day, but there was almost no automobile traffic out on Brookstown Avenue, as snow had been falling for hours. Most of the neighborhood businesses were closed, except for the Rainbow, one block over on Summit Avenue. Most of the people who worked there lived within easy walking distance, as I did from my office. I had left my car at home.

The snow had stopped falling by early morning, and the sun shone brightly in a crystal-blue sky, but only a few hardy pedestrians were out and about. One of their number had stopped on the sidewalk across from our building, I noticed. Glancing up from my desk, I saw that he was looking directly at me, framed as I was by the panorama of windows and illuminated by track lights showing off the Jargon folk-art collection.

This unfamiliar pedestrian appeared to be about my size and age. With snowflakes dusting his medium-length blond hair, he wore an olive-drab coverall that looked practical for the weather, as did his leather gloves and heavy-duty, lace-up boots. He waved, a half-smile on his good-looking face, and mimed a request to come inside. I returned the wave and motioned to the entrance on the back side of the building, where he headed upon crossing the street.

Opening the door, he stomped the snow off his boots, stepped inside, and introduced himself:

"Snow. John Snow."

Identifying himself as an artist, John Snow inquired about the art he'd seen from the street, so I gave him a quick tour. As he inspected the premises I sensed that the visionary folk art was a bit raw for his refined tastes—a current of snobbishness beneath his friendly demeanor.

Obviously wondering who I was and what I represented, he was more interested in the books I showed him, including the newly published *White Trash Cooking*.

"Oh yes, I've heard about this one," he told me as he flipped through a copy. "There was a review on NPR. Very amusing!"

He claimed to be aware of Jonathan Williams, with whom he said he shared mutual friends, but didn't recall ever meeting him. I told him a little about the books I was working on with Jonathan.

In my capsule history of the Jargon Society I mentioned Buckminster Fuller, whose *Epic Poem on the History of Industrialization* Jonathan published in the early 1960s. This piqued my visitor's interest. He said he'd been reading Fuller's magnum opus, *Synergetics* and conducting his own experiments with the tetrahedron or triangular pyramid, Fuller's model of the simplest possible form.

"You must come over to my studio and see my tetrahedrons. I've built some big ones out of bamboo."

He told me a little about his studio.

"It's at the end of Brookstown Avenue, just this side of Old Salem. Two stories above ground, red-brick exterior—a triangular building, like the Flatiron Building in New York. It used to be headquarters for the family business, Snow Electric Company, and not long ago it was an art gallery. The upstairs is my studio."

"I've noticed it driving by," I told him. "I'd like to see the inside. And the bamboo tetrahedrons."

Offering John a chair, I sat down at my desk and swiveled around so I faced him. He asked if he could smoke, and I said sure, moving an ashtray within arms length and sliding a Camel Light from the pack in my shirt pocket.

"I see you smoke one of our local brands," he observed as he fished a pack of rolling papers and a paper pouch of Drum tobacco from one his coveralls. "I prefer to roll my own." Which he proceeded to do, using an otherwise empty space at the edge of my desk. The rolling of smokeable material in a licked cigarette paper introduced the subject of pot-smoking, albeit euphemistically.

"Yes," John Snow mused as he exhaled an even stream of smoke from his pointed nose, "I'm glad to see you enjoy tobacco like I do. And maybe you smoke other materials as well. I find that as an artist I benefit especially from art supplies, if you know what I mean. Maybe it's the same for you as a writer. I'll bet you like to have art supplies on hand. For inspiration, I mean." Air quotes implied.

"Art supplies," I repeated. "Uh.... oh, yes, indeed." I replied. "Essential! Art supplies!."

John Snow flashed a knowing smile and nodded. Without mentioning cannabis by any of its usual street names, he let me know that he was well-connected in that department—in case I found the information useful.

"Well, as a matter of fact," I offered, "I might have some art supplies with me. Let's get away from my window on the world for a minute so I can let you sample them. A special batch I acquired in Atlanta."

And so we ducked into one of the back rooms, where I pushed a window open a few inches to vent any residual smoke. I filled my little pipe, and we passed it back and forth, inhaling deeply, trying not to cough, until the sample was incinerated.

To clarify, John Snow was not a drug dealer, but he seemed to enjoy being a potential facilitator. Hence his offer to connect me, if needed, with a supplier of our favorite smokable plant.

Whatever else he might have been, he was a bright conversationalist with an interesting history. He told me he'd been a religion-studies major at Wake Forest University and had spent several years studying painting in Philadelphia, at the venerable Pennsylvania Academy of Fine Arts. He was thirty-five, and he'd been back in his hometown for a decade by the time I arrived.

Soon after that fortuitously timed snow-day meeting John invited me to visit his studio. He encouraged me to bring Diana, whom I'd mentioned.

*

The Flatiron Building, as John insisted on calling it, was hemmed in on all three sides. Marshall Street, a major artery from downtown, marked the property's western boundary, and Wachovia Street bounded it on the southeast. A patch of dirt on the Brookstown Avenue side was barely large enough to accommodate a couple of small cars and a pile of firewood alongside a wooden door marked with the address, number 300, stencil-painted on a brick wall about half covered with English ivy.

The main ground-floor entrance was a set of double doors inset with a row of windowpanes near the top, on the east corner facing Old Salem. The Brookstown door, windowless wood, was a back entrance that gave direct access to the ground floor and a broad, heavily worn, wooden staircase to the open second floor—a cavernous, high-ceilinged, brick-walled room with heavy wooden rafters and vertical beams supporting the roof.

The building was zoned for business use only, not as residential property. John officially lived with his widowed mother in the Buena Vista neighborhood, bastion of the local gentry, but he seemed to spend most of his time, day or night, in the studio at the Flatiron.

His studio was as a veritable cabinet of curiosities, as imaginatively cluttered as Howard Finster's garden. Except for a ragtag assortment of second- or third-hand furniture including several comfortable armchairs and spatially disorienting mirrors, the cavernous, high-ceilinged room was mostly filled with paintings, sculptures, and other things John had made. In addition to the bamboo tetrahedrons—two of them, each about seven feet tall—there were some large landscape paintings, a few smaller portrait heads, and lots of insect-like forms made from cut and folded pink paper suspended like Calder mobiles from the ceiling.

The paintings were mostly landscapes—the largest depicting a placeless volcano—with lots of painterly, impressionistic visual drama in prevailing shades of pink and blue with tinges of yellow. Large sections of the rough brick walls on which they hung were covered with aluminum foil, some areas of which had been painted freehand with decorative, symmetrical scrollwork. This was evidently a graphic specialty, as similar patterns enlivened some of the paper insects and many of the found objects scattered about the place. Stylized masks were worked into some of these neo-baroque designs.

Parts of the wall in the studio's eastern corner were encrusted with tiny assemblages and collages made from photos of John and other people I didn't recognize, in some cases wearing few if any clothes. By day the room was amply illuminated by natural light streaming into tall, narrow windows whose glass panes were decorated with more painted scrollwork.

On the westernmost corners of both floors were restrooms consisting of a toilet and sink in matching rusted porcelain. The restroom at the bottom of the stairs was enclosed and had a door that could be locked from inside. Unselfconscious guests and exhibitionists were free to use the unenclosed upstairs facilities.

On the opposite side of the studio, in the social space near the big window above the double-doored main entrance, was a wood stove whose vertical smoke-exhaust pipe right-angled through a foil-sheathed hole in the wall behind it. Since it was wintertime and the studio was occupied, the stove was stoked, radiating heat that was somewhat contained by long sheets of semi-transparent plastic hung from the rafters near that end of the room.

Suspended from a rafter near the center of the studio was a chromed metal ring the size of a hula hoop. It was ideally positioned for doing chin-ups or practicing acrobatic moves, which could also be performed on the big tetrahedrons.   Almost within reach of this silver ring was a tall stepladder whose upper end was propped against the inside of a trap door opening to the building's flat tar roof.

"The Flatiron was originally the power-station for Winston and Salem back in the late nineteenth century," John explained. "Electrical power was routed to the building from the Yadkin River Dam, and from here it was distributed to the local factories and homes and businesses."

In 1987 the building was still owned by John's family, and the bottom floor was rental property, unoccupied at the time of my first visit. John showed it to us, but we spent most of our time upstairs, where the air was dense with smoke and classical music from the FM station at Wake Forest. Obviously curious about Diana and me—

two characters previously unknown to him—John grilled us for personal information, and he shared gossip about local characters we knew only slightly if at all.

Intensely self-centered, John Snow was a guy who clearly felt himself on top of it all—smarter and more talented than anyone in rock-throwing range. He struck me early on as gay, although he made multiple references to his girlfriends and seemed intent on projecting an image as an equal-opportunity libertine. He flagrantly flirted with Diana, and he seemed to get a kick out of "tweaking" anyone in his presence, probing us for weaknesses and sensitivities he could use to "push our buttons"—a favorite phrase in his vocabulary.

In any case, John made for interesting company. We cultivated each other over the next few years and met each other's friends. His studio became a regular stop on my itinerary for out-of-town guests and visitors. It was also the setting for casual personal visits and long discussions about mutual interests, not to mention occasional personal dramas.

Not long after I'd met John I brought Jonathan and Tom over one evening to meet him and see his studio. They were cordial enough, but I don't think they were terribly impressed.

29. A HOT GOLDEN CHARIOT

Of course I had no intention of letting my work on the Finster book go to waste. Nor would I squander any energy cursing John Turner or resenting Jonathan's abrupt change of tune about the project. Jonathan didn't deny he'd been fickle on this score, and he was clearly dismayed by the apparent impasse that confronted me in the wake of Turner's about-face and independent contractual dealings. So, when he suggested New York literary agent Irene Skolnick might be a good one to scout a new publisher, I gamely accepted an introduction. Irene was employed by the Wallace & Sheil agency and had assisted Jargon's recent negotiations with Ten Speed Press.

Details of Irene's talks with publishers amount to inside baseball, but the process took a couple of years and is easily summarized for present purposes: Abbeville Press, a division of legendary art-book publisher Harry Abrams, eventually stepped forward to take on the Finster project, which became a four-way collaboration with Howard, Roger Manley, and Victor Faccinto. To augment Roger's and Victor's photographs, we were given unrestricted access to the slide archives of Phyllis Kind and Cavin-Morris, the two New York galleries that had shown Finster's art.

Cut loose from the Jargon Society in mid-summer of

'87, and financially buoyed by the advance for the EOM book, I focused on completing the Finster manuscript by year's end. Accordingly, I planned to spend a week in Georgia, determined to nail down a few last details that remained fuzzy in the free-ranging autobiographical narrative Howard had shared with me in bits and pieces.

Chief among these was his preaching history. On many occasions Howard had referenced the ten different churches he'd led in northwest Georgia and northeast Alabama. I felt it was important to establish an accurate chronology of his time at these rural and small-town churches. Knowing him as well as I did, I figured he was unlikely to lay it out for me in a neat summary, so I suggested we spend a day driving to see these venerable institutions firsthand, beginning with his first church and following in chronological order. It was the only way I could think of to keep him focused on the subject.

In preparation for the trip, I phoned my friend Roger Dorset—himself a brilliant, idiosyncratic artist, formally trained—to see if he might put me up for a few nights at his place in Rome, Georgia, about an hour's drive south of Paradise Garden. Having repeatedly immersed myself in "Finsterland" over seven years, I felt I needed a quieter setting to gather my thoughts and type up my notes between sessions with Howard.

In addition to his suburban ranch house filled with

his own art and collected artifacts, Roger Dorset kept a fully-furnished, art-festooned apartment in a nearby building of rental properties he'd inherited from an aunt. He offered the apartment to me gratis for the duration of my stay. With these arrangements in place, I packed a few belongings, including my 1939 Royal typewriter, and drove down from Winston-Salem. The aim was to fill in the remaining gaps in my manuscript, which by that time I'd largely assembled as a running narrative.

Howard was nostalgic about his years as a church pastor, and he readily agreed to my suggestion that we visit his former places of religious employment. None was more than an hour's drive from the Garden, but visiting them all was bound to occupy an entire day.

So enthusiastic was Howard about this outing that he insisted on driving. He'd recently purchased a used, gold-hued Cadillac, in which he promised we could travel in style.

It had been two years since Howard's commissioned painting graced the cover of Talking Heads' award-winning *Little Creatures* LP. Thus alerted to his work, droves of twenty-something rock fans and art students had been frequenting Paradise Garden. More than a few of them camped out for several days at a time while volunteering their labor, mostly on the tiered tower atop the World's Folk Art Church—still a work in progress.

On the scene in this capacity during my visit was Fred Leighton, an art student from Miami University in Ohio. He asked if he might join Howard and me for our church tour, and of course we welcomed him aboard.

The summer weather was typically sweltering in Georgia, but Howard dressed up for the occasion—dark suit, white dress shirt, and snazzy necktie. It wasn't until we were en route that we realized the golden chariot's air-conditioner was on the fritz. So the three of us spent the entire day sweating profusely in whatever we happened to be wearing—jeans and a t-shirt for me—as Howard chauffeured us around Southern Appalachia's Valley and Ridge Mountains, stopping periodically so he could show us the churches where he formerly occupied the pulpit. It was a weekday, so none of them were open, but he posed for photographs in front of each one, and of course he had stories to tell in every case.

After completing the church tour, and since it was on our way, we wrapped up the day's excursion with a visit to an old cemetery where members of Howard's family were buried. It was there that I photographed Howard posed over the tombstone of his sister Abbie Rose Finster, who died at thirteen, from a toxic reaction to rabies shots administered following a dog attack.

It was Abbie, Howard recalled, who appeared to him in his inaugural vision, when he was only three years old. On many occasions he'd described her descent from a staircase in the sky, whereupon she foretold the special mission he was to fulfill on Earth.

30. A BOOK TO DIE FOR

The Southern Visionary Folk Art Preservation Project ground to a halt on schedule, July 1987. I wrapped up my administrative work for the Jargon Society and returned to full-time freelance writing, the occupation I'd been pursuing in Atlanta when my wild Jargon ride began. I gradually moved out of the Brookstown Avenue office, a few pieces of furniture and art at a time. Most of the stuff remained in situ for someone else to deal with. Jonathan returned to his nominal role as Jargon's executive director, albeit without doing anything different from what he'd long been doing. He continued to preside over this curious cultural enterprise from his lofty perch in the Nantahala Mountains—"in the azure, over the squalor."

Notwithstanding his withdrawal of support for the Finster book, I was grateful to Jonathan for the confidence he'd shown in me at a pivotal moment. There was no question that my three-year experience with his maverick publishing outfit lent me some new cachet and career visibility.

I thought about moving back to Atlanta, which in many ways still felt like home. On the other hand, I'd accustomed myself to Winston-Salem—a town I found agreeable, where living expenses were far lower than Atlanta's and traffic far less maddening, and where interesting company was not hard to come by. Only a five-hour drive down I-85, Atlanta was a city of enduring friendships and cultural opportunities, so I maintained my ties there by continuing to visit several times a year.

Meanwhile, Atlanta-based *Art Papers*—which had years earlier nudged me into writing about art—tapped me to become its new North Carolina editor, enabling me to assign regional reviews and feature articles to other writers and, occasionally, to myself. The gig brought me a monthly editorial stipend in addition to fees for my own pieces. Income also trickled in from catalog essays I wrote to accompany gallery shows, and from occasional talks I continued to give about visionary folk art.

Late in the year, 1987, after what seemed like a long wait, *St. EOM in the Land of Pasaquan*, finally materialized, with an official publication date of October thirty-first, Halloween.

Boo!

Four thousand copies of a red clothbound edition with eye-catching slipcover, priced at thirty bucks, and 100 copies of a special, black-boxed patrons' edition, to be numbered and signed by me and the three principal photographers—JW, Roger Manley, and Guy Mendes. Special price for prescient patrons: $100!

In September, as a prelude to publication, Piedmont Craftsmen Gallery, in the heart of downtown Winston-

Salem, premiered an exhibition of EOM's paintings, homemade costumes, and other hand-crafted artifacts. This curatorial collaboration with Fred Fussell was the result of that Southern Arts Federation grant, which also entailed subsequent bookings of the show.

On a Saturday in late autumn I convened with Jonathan, Roger, and Guy to sign the EOM patrons' edition at the Captain's Bookshelf in Asheville—Jonathan's birth city. Captain's was an exceptional establishment specializing in used and rare books. I had known proprietors Chan and Miegan Gordon for ten years, and Jonathan had known them even longer. Despite the necessarily compact space, it was an institution—a bastion of cultural literacy in a town that had seen better days. The shop was a perfect match for Jargon's culturally subversive press and EOM's free-ranging spirit.

There were plates of custom-baked cookies, artfully configured in the form of a Pasaquoyanized yin-yang symbol, with red and yellow icing to match the book cover's predominant colors. Jonathan arrived peering out from a plastic Richard Nixon Halloween mask, which we took turns wearing as we signed the book, each using a different color ink. We also autographed copies of the regular edition purchased by visitors.

A few weeks later I signed and inscribed copies of the regular edition at Winston-Salem's Rainbow News and

Cafe, which had moved about half a mile to the east, into a converted, two-story house on Brookstown Avenue. And in early 1988 I did likewise at Atlanta's Oxford Bookstore, where a crowd of old friends turned out and scores of copies were sold. The Atlanta event also occasioned a visit with Hunter, my brother and lifelong comrade-in-arms, who lived near the store and hosted me for a few days.

*

John Russell's introduction to the EOM book no doubt helped catch the attention of the *New York Times Book Review*, in which Peter Schjeldahl waxed enthusiastic: "There is no cog on the ratchet of American rugged individualism beyond that of St. EOM, and his disaffected creative drive is archetypal for much that is strong in American art."

National Public Radio aired a segment about the book, mostly consisting of an interview that the local-affiliate's ace reporter Paul Brown conducted with me one afternoon in Winston-Salem.

There were rave blurbs aplenty.

"As the gutsiest mixture of folk art and autobiography imaginable, this opens epic vistas as wide and as old as grass-roots America," announced art historian Robert Rosenblum.

"*St. EOM* is an evocative thing, evidence that Eddie Martin was at least the equal of Simon Rodia of the Watts

Towers," commented *Blue Highways* author William Least Heat Moon.

Writing in the New York weekly *Paper*, poet and art dealer Randall Morris hailed *St. EOM* as an important book that "finally and with a sure hand subverts and devastates the public conception of the self-taught artist as naive, primitive, sweet, and isolated from the moral seriousness of the 'real' world." Summarizing EOM as "a combination of Rimbaud, Genet and Lou Reed," Morris described him as "a storyteller and a rhythmic genius conveying the pulse of the mean streets and the role of the constantly crucified hustler in words sinewy and vivid."

"The man…can be elegant and fine as Chinese bronze, and lusty and vulgar as a moose in heat," wrote poet Jeffery Beam. "His eloquence denies no one entrance into his world if the reader/viewer is equal to his contradictory and individual outlook…." Beam summed it up as a "fascinating, demanding and sometimes overwhelming book."

"Jeez, the old boy was really onto somethin', wasn't he!" novelist and essayist Ed McClanahan observed.

Nary a discouraging word.

Aside from raising my own profile a few notches, all the attention could only help ensure the preservation of EOM's self-designed temple compound, a wonder of the Weird South—way, way, way out there.

31. BEYOND JARGON

It would take years for the regular edition of *St. EOM* to sell out, but the book made a splash in the big pond of American art in the Funless Eighties. Personally, it would be hard to top—a career high, perhaps achieved too soon.

As a friend in New Orleans told me, "Man, you write a book like that, you can die!"

But of course I lived on, kept finding things to write about, and continued to require a modest income. Fortunately the media buzz about *St. EOM* helped me get my next couple of jobs.

To wit: Early in 1988 the local daily *Winston-Salem Journal* recruited me to write a weekly column about visual art for the Sunday edition. A motivating factor, I later learned, was a widely circulated petition lobbying features editor Joe Goodman to hire a qualified art critic— whatever "qualified" might have meant at the time.

John Snow—he of the baby Flatiron Building and the bamboo tetrahedrons—got wind of the campaign and commenced dropping cryptic presentiments regarding the important role I would soon come to play in the community.

And lo, it came to pass…..

In this new capacity I was expected to review and comment on art exhibitions in Winston-Salem, elsewhere in North Carolina, and sometimes farther afield. I was generally free to choose my subjects, with the stipulation that any exhibition I wrote about must be on view for a week or more beyond the publication date. I was encouraged to cast a consistent critical eye. And I had to arrange for photos of relevant art to accompany the column, either supplied by the host venues or made on assignment by the newspaper's staff photographers. I was told I needed a name for the column, so I named it "Eye on Art."

No sooner had I signed on to be the *Winston-Salem Journal*'s official art eyeball than I was cruised by the Asheville-based *Arts Journal*—a struggling, non-profit, monthly tabloid magazine that was about $1,000 in debt for each of the dozen years it had been in existence. They were looking for a new editor.

I had been aware of the *AJ* almost since the beginning and had occasionally read items of interest published in its pages. I had pegged it as an artsy-craftsy regional rag with a backwoods-hippie vibe, so I was a little surprised to learn that the North Carolina Arts Council classified it as a statewide arts resource—a status that came with several thousand Arts Council dollars every year, not to be sneezed at.

I was also surprised at the enthusiastic response to my casual inquiry about the editorial job. I had mailed it shortly before agreeing to the local art column.

I could think of a million ways to improve the *Arts Journal* and make it more interesting and relevant for a broader audience, I told Myron Gauger, the publication's board president, when he drove down the mountain one day in the spring to talk with me about the job—a salaried, full-time position with health insurance.

Myron was a wiry, compact, soft-spoken guy with neatly trimmed hair and a full, graying beard. He was a sculptor, drove a GMC pickup truck, and didn't pretend to know more than he did about art or anything else—an intelligent non-intellectual. I liked him from the outset, but I could tell we were on different wave-lengths.

The *Arts Journal*'s accumulated debt left me skittish, but I figured it was the responsibility of the board, not a freshly hired editor. So I cast aside any misgivings and took the job.

Maybe I was expected to give up the weekly newspaper column I'd just begun to write, and it was probably assumed I would move to Asheville. I did neither such thing. Nineteen grand a year plus medical insurance sounded good, but as long as the *AJ* remained deeply in debt, I would consider my editorial job tenuous—reason enough to stay in Winston for the time being. The art-column was piecework, but it was regular piecework, and it seemed like a more stable position. I had no desire to live full-time in Asheville, something of a backwater in those days, with a thriving community of retirees but not much to show for itself culturally except the semi-restored house where Thomas Wolfe grew up.

Suddenly, then—going into the spring—I had a full-time job and a part-time job in two different cities. Two different worlds, really, although separated by only 150 miles. And for a couple of years I managed to keep a foot in each one.

32. BIG PLAYER

It seemed plenty ironic that I'd concluded my intensive work in the visionary folk art field just as art museums and other institutions around the country were taking a stronger interest. Among the early signs of the latter trend was an important exhibition that opened in Atlanta that spring and ran through the summer.

"Outside the Mainstream: Folk Art in Our Time" was curated by Barbara Archer, the education coordinator at the High Museum of Art. A North Carolina native, she had contacted me a few years earlier at the Jargon office. I'd shown her the Jargon collection and taken her to visit James Harold Jennings' roadside art environment.

Barbara's show—at the High's freshly minted downtown branch, in the Georgia-Pacific corporation's new office tower—brought together works by sixty contemporary self-taught artists from all over the southeastern United States, including most of the "Southern Visionary Folk Artists" Roger Manley and I had exhibited in 1985. Other featured artists had been more recently documented and introduced to the art world by Judith McWillie and William Arnett, who'd attended my slide talk in Marietta the previous year.

McWillie and Arnett were no longer collaborating, for reasons beyond the scope of this account, but they both continued to focus on black vernacular art. While Judith channeled her early research into an exhibition and accompanying catalog at New York's INTAR Latin American Gallery (*Another Face of the Diamond: Pathways through the Black Atlantic South,* 1988), Bill emerged as a major collector and dealer in this subset of the field. At his invitation, Jonathan Williams joined him for a couple of art-seeking road trips that became fodder for essays in JW's *Big Book of Southern Folk Art.*

Having negotiated exclusive contracts to represent a number of important self-taught black artists in the growing outsider-art market, Arnett had loaned major works to "Outside the Mainstream" from the vast collection he'd begun to assemble at his sprawling home in Atlanta's upscale Buckhead district, one block from the Georgia Governor's Mansion.

In conjunction with the exhibition's opening Arnett hosted a huge party, with many of the featured artists in attendance, along with a few hundred Atlanta art-scene makers. It was a lovely spring night among the magnolias, and I stayed for hours, talking with most of the special guests—Thornton Dial, Bessie Harvey, Lonnie Holley, Charlie Lucas, Archie Byron, and Mose Tolliver, along with various members of their families.

During a tête-à-tête with Bessie Harvey I pulled a notebook from my gas-mask bag, intending to write down something insightful she'd said. Glancing at a free-form drawing I'd made on the random page to which I opened it, she exclaimed, "That looks just like one of my pieces!"

So it did, I confirmed, studying it as if I'd never seen it before.

During much of the evening Mose Tolliver held court in the Arnetts' kitchen, where I hung out with him for a while and, at his request, kept refilling his plastic cup with beer from one of the kegs in the adjacent carport. It was only later that I was informed he wasn't supposed to be drinking alcohol.

It was an evening to remember. Energized by the lively conversation and remarkable art on view throughout the house, I stayed into the wee hours. One of the last guests on the premises, I spent my final minutes in conversation with Bill Arnett, mostly listening while he spoke expansively and extravagantly about the artists he'd been cultivating.

"Thornton Dial is a genius, greater than Picasso!" He thundered. "He's as great as Van Gogh or Leonardo!"

Suddenly exhausted, I was making my way to my car, and Bill was following me, caught up in the vortex of his harangue. I had no mind to argue with him, and I certainly wouldn't have denied the greatness of Dial or any of the other artists he'd begun to champion. I just didn't think it was useful to make all these grand art-historical pronouncements. Bill had transformed into a nuisance salesman, and I was feeling besieged. I was ready to call it a night—or an early morning, still pitch-dark except for a streetlight beam piercing the greenery. I needed to get some sleep and spend a day or two thinking about what I'd just experienced.

Following along and likewise involved in the discussion with Bill was his new assistant Xenia Zed, a longtime friend and colleague who'd recently left the editor's chair at *Art Papers*. Xenia and I went way back, as veteran assistants to Judith Alexander, whose Atlanta gallery was past tense by this time. We knew our Atlanta folk-art history.

Probably sensing my discomfort and mounting exasperation with her boss, Xenia was trying to bring it all to a lighthearted conclusion, but to no avail. Bill was still yelling as I got into my car and drove away, waving goodbye out the open window.

"Bill Arnett's like that character played by Wallace Beery in the old movie," Jonathan Williams later commented.

"'I'm the only white man the natives trust!' he says as he makes his way out of the jungle."

33. OUT TO LUNCH

Headquartered near the end of Charlotte Street, in a little stone building that had originally been the real-estate office of E.W. Grove— developer of the nearby Grove Park Inn—the *Arts Journal* was a technologically primitive labor of love. The typography was input by keyboard directly into a clunky old compositor that was about ten years out of date, probably emitting toxic fumes as it spit out ragged-edged columns with annoying spatial glitches. The layout, meanwhile, was cluttered with clever but superfluous doodle sketches by the publication's longtime art director, who happened to be the typographer's significant other. The two co-workers shared an apartment and were sometimes at each other's throats. They drank, and they smoked cigarettes, but not to complain, because in those days so did I. Personally I liked them both.

Our skeletal staff literally took the publication to press every month—hand-carried it, or rather transported it by car, to nearby Waynesville, where the hometown newspaper essentially rented its in-house web press and line staff to us for the day. They charged a reasonable fee for production, including the newsprint our little rag was printed on. At the end of the day we loaded up the heavy stacks of new issues and drove them back to the office in

Asheville for distribution to subscribers, advertisers, and newsstands.

I began my tenure with the *AJ* in May, and the June 1988 issue was the first under my editorial direction. I quickly realized I could perform most of my editorial and grant-writing chores from my home desk, and was needed in the Asheville office mainly during the two weeks leading up to our press deadline. In Winston-Salem the only time I spent in the local newsroom was the hour it took me each week to retype my marked-up typescript column for "input" into the newspaper's computer system—a task I performed on any keyboard that happened to be free when I dropped by, usually on Mondays. Early submissions were always welcome, and sometimes delivered, depending on other commitments. I never submitted my copy late.

To accommodate the *Arts Journal*'s press schedule I found a small, cheap, furnished apartment in Asheville while retaining my secluded Winston-Salem digs, behind the larger, two-story unit occupied by significant other Diana and her avian sidekick, Buzzy the Amazon parrot. Diana had her own schedule and her art studio—her own world, really—and didn't seem to mind too much my monthly absences during the Asheville intervals.

Like the handful of other staffers, all members of the *AJ*'s board of directors lived in Asheville and vicinity, so my time there enabled me to attend meetings of the full board and some of its various committees.

It was a strange time in my professional life. No longer employed by the Jargon Society, I knew my reputation—such as it was—was largely based on the work I'd done on Jargon's behalf, especially the St. EOM book.

Eddie Martin had been dead for two years by the time I said yes to the *Arts Journal*, but his spirit still hovered over some of my activities.

The Seattle trip, for instance.

*

The Saint EOM exhibition Fred Fussell and I co-curated under the Southern Arts Federation's auspices was still on tour. To fill a summer slot beginning in early July, the director of the Center on Contemporary Art (CoCA) in Seattle—a wiry, eternally wired art punk named Larry Reid—booked our exhibition to share a double-bill with a show of "shotgun paintings" and stenciled spray-paint imagery by William Burroughs. By prior arrangement I flew across the country to attend the opening reception and related events, including a joint book-signing with Burroughs, a hero of my youth.

At sixteen, in 1968, I brought the Grove Press paperback edition of *Naked Lunch* to my public high school in small-town Georgia every day for the week or two I spent reading it. Just for fun I read selected passages aloud during lunch breaks, alternately disgusting, amusing, and befuddling my classmates gathered around a cast-concrete picnic table in the parking lot next to the cafeteria.

Twenty years later I found myself on a July evening at a special table in the Elliott Bay Bookstore, Seattle's leading literary venue, alongside William Burroughs. Roger Manley and I were there to sign copies of *St. EOM in the Land of Pasaquan*, and Burroughs to sign…. whatever his disciples brought him, including every dusty, dog-eared paperback copy of *Naked Lunch* for miles around.

The disciples were out in force—the gaunt, the goth, and the grunged-out, the strange, and the strung-out— lined up through the store and out the door, stretched around half of the big city block. Some of them picked up copies of the newest book, *The Western Lands*, on their way in to meet the gray-eminence junkie survivor, who blessed them by inscribing their books.

I didn't mind being heavily overshadowed and upstaged. Although he'd pegged himself in print as *el Hombre Invisible*, the moniker hardly applied anymore. A walking, snarling counterculture icon, Burroughs had become instantly recognizable. He was a Beat celebrity, every would-be hipster's weird old uncle.

And so, from our ringside seats, Roger and I enjoyed watching Uncle Bill interact with his devotees as he autographed at least 100 books for every copy of *St. EOM* we signed.

The book-signing was the first of several events we would attend with Burroughs and his assistant James Grauerholz during that week in Seattle. Burroughs would give a reading before a packed auditorium downtown on Saturday evening, and in the meantime there was the opening reception at CoCA, where a regional group show was on view in addition to the Burroughs and EOM exhibitions.

Hundreds of people turned out for the opening, including Roger Manley's parents—coincidentally visiting the Great Northwest with a tour group— and the avant-garde artist duo of Ed and Nancy Kienholz. The Keinholzes lived in nearby Idaho and were old friends of Burroughs through the Beat network. A longtime admirer of their work, I was thrilled at the opportunity to meet them.

On Sunday Burroughs was the guest of honor at a ticketed outdoor picnic lunch, at which all were rather modestly clothed, notwithstanding the perfect weather. "Lunch with William Burroughs" was followed by an afternoon of lectures and a panel discussion at the University of Washington. As a teaser for Burroughs' extemporaneous talk about his paintings, I gave a slide presentation on Saint EOM, the spoken component of which consisted mostly of quoted passages from his street-life memoir.

"You sound just like him!" Burroughs said to me afterward, as if he'd known Eddie. Not entirely out of the question.

It wasn't the first time I'd crossed paths with William Burroughs, and it wouldn't be the last.

34. CULTURE WARS

A few days after the Seattle summit I was back in North Carolina, neck-deep in the regional art scene. Navigating my new responsibilities as a critic and arts editor would have required quick study and on-the-job learning under any circumstances. I plunged in during what would prove to be a historical turning-point—the beginning of the Culture Wars—so the transition was intense.

It was the season when self-appointed guardians of morality and religion launched a frontal attack on the American art system. Commencing that summer with a nationwide campaign to boycott and picket theaters showing Martin Scorsese's *The Last Temptation of Christ,* it escalated over the ensuing months and years as these censorious forces bore down on contemporary visual art and its public-support structure.

In early 1989 they discovered Andres Serrano, a federally funded artist who'd made a photograph they deemed sacrilegious, and Robert Mapplethorpe, another New York photographer, whose touring retrospective show was about to open at D.C.'s Corcoran Gallery of Art. The Mapplethorpe exhibition included a few homoerotic images that inflamed the mob, so the Corcoran hastily called the whole thing off.

Originating in the South—no surprise—the torch-wielding parade was led by U.S. Senator Jesse Helms and the director of the Mississippi-based American Family Association, one Donald Wildmon. Touting traditional family values, they emerged brandishing the Good Book, the favored weapon in their War on Art.

As the denouement to the Funless Eighties, this clash of viewpoints became the overriding story for almost anyone engaged with art in the U.S.A. It formed the broader cultural context of my time with the *Arts Journal*, headquartered in Jesse Helms' home state. So of course it was reflected in the content of the magazine.

My first salvo was a scathing editorial in the September '88 issue, prompted by the outcry over *The Last Temptation*. In May of '89, I used my editorial forum to criticize state legislators seeking drastic cuts in the North Carolina Arts Council's budget, and in August I took on the so-called religious right for the attack on Serrano and the Mapplethorpe show's cancellation.

By the end of 1989 the *Arts Journal* continued to cast a broad net for content, but almost every issue made reference to the ongoing conflict. This trend was driven not so much by editorial choice as by current events and the related concerns of our writers, all of whom held strong views on the subjects of art and free expression.

Perhaps all too predictably, the *Arts Journal*'s steady

monitoring of these issues became a point of contention with the board, whose members generally advocated a more boosterish stance for the magazine. Some of them seemed to see it strictly as a promotional outlet for our wonderful state where we cared so much about art!

The way I saw it, if we cared so much about art we needed to speak up when it was under attack.

As a non-profit organization, we were legally forbidden from political involvement, but that was usually taken to mean partisan politics. For me and most of the artists and writers I knew, there was nothing partisan about the issue. In a democratic society—small 'd'—free expression was fundamental.

*

The front line in the mounting Culture Wars was drawn almost literally across my own backyard. As the largest and most influential art institution in Winston-Salem, the Southeastern Center for Contemporary Art would have been centrally positioned on my local art-critic radar in any case. But it was forcibly thrust to the center by the big, bold target painted on its back by the new national art police.

SECCA's cardinal sin was honoring Andres Serrano's work, and especially—notoriously—Serrano's"crucifix-submerged-in-urine" photograph with the memorable title *Piss Christ*. A beautiful, heroically scaled photograph, it was included in a traveling show spotlighting Serrano's work and that of other recipients of SECCA's national Awards in the Visual Arts (AVA). The exhibition never appeared at SECCA—or anywhere else in North Carolina, for that matter—and Serrano's photograph drew only one viewer complaint at the final venue on the national tour.

That was all it took. Ignited by sensationalist publicity, "Piss Christ" became the fuse that lit the bomb that kept going off. SECCA would suffer for years to come, in many ways, but the fallout was far more widespread.

35. PRIMATES

I don't know the circumstances of what was presumably a family decision, but at some point in the late 1980s, the retail space that had been advertised on the ground floor of Winston-Salem's mini-Flatiron Building was withdrawn from the local rental market. John Snow cleared it out, cleaned it up, and transformed it into a raw space for art exhibitions. He hosted only a couple before he scrapped the idea.

The first was a solo show by Diana Dorn, my significant other. Her laminated drawings and loose-canvas paintings were mounted on the brick walls and hung from a clothesline-like configuration of heavy string stretched in zig-zag fashion across the center of the room. The exhibit opened on her thirty-sixth birthday, but if you blinked you missed it, because it closed two days later.

I was still the North Carolina editor of *Art Papers*, and despite the clear conflict of interest I submitted a review. Glenn Harper was the magazine's relatively new executive editor, Xenia Zed having moved on to work with Bill Arnett.

"Never write about an artist's work if you've slept with them in the last twenty-four hours," Glenn declared, laughing. Then he published my review.

*

A couple of months later Diana and I were visiting John at his studio on a summer night after drinks at a nearby bar. I spontaneously decided to do a few acrobatic turns on one of the bamboo tetrahedrons, not for the first time.

Standing in the center of the open, three-sided pyramid, I reached both hands up and grabbed two of the intersecting poles near the apex, then I swung my head and shoulders backward while lifting my ankles high.

I guess my hands were slippery with sweat, because I lost my grip on the smooth wood, plummeting to the floor to land on my back, hard enough to knock the breath out of me.

Wheezing loudly, I struggled to my feet and staggered across the room to stop Diana, who was about to phone 911.

"No! No!" I wheezed. "I'm fine, *wheeze wheeze*, really, *wheeze*, I'm fine."

Diana and John were both certain I'd hurt myself seriously enough to call for an ambulance. Of course he didn't say it, but John was probably even more worried about a lawsuit. But as I gradually regained my breath and my equilibrium, I assured my companions I was intact. To demonstrate my quick recovery I strode back and forth across the room, then I spun myself around a couple of turns before walking briskly down and back up the stairs.

The next morning I woke up in excruciating pain. It was rare for me to take so much as an aspirin, but in this case I felt like I might need something stronger, so I drove to a nearby drugstore. On a pharmacist's recommendation I bought a name-brand ibuprofen, a drug I'd never tried before. I had to drive to Asheville that afternoon. Fortunately the ibuprofen completely numbed the injury, and I made the two-hour drive without thinking about the mishap.

A few days later I phoned Charlotte Hanes, nee Metz, who'd been married to Philip for a year or two by that time, and who—to remind—was a physical therapist by profession. I told her about my fall from the bamboo tetrahedron and tried to describe the pain I was still experiencing and its location in my lower back region. She asked me a few questions, and she left me with some words of sensible advice.

"People are all the time telling me, 'It hurts when I do this,'" she explained. "And they'll try to show me by moving their arm or their leg in a certain way. And I just tell them, 'Then don't do that!'" So if there are any kind of movements that you find are irritating to that part of your back, avoid them."

*

In April 1989 I crossed paths again with William Burroughs. As in our recent Seattle encounter, Roger

Manley was involved, and this time John Snow was along for the ride.

The occasion was a reading by Allen Ginsberg at Duke University, which I learned about from Burroughs' assistant James Grauerholz. James was a contemporary and an ideal go-between for Burroughs in his dealings with the public—very bright, even-tempered, and (just in case) big and physically strong-looking. He phoned me in March and told me William had decided to fly to Durham to see his old friend, and to take care of some other business.

William was working on a book set in Madagascar, James explained—*Ghost of Chance*, it was titled. Madagascar is famous for its unique native population of lemurs, which figure into the narrative. It's the only place to see lemurs in the wild except for Duke University's Primate Center, on the outskirts of Durham, where several different kinds of lemurs were studied in luxurious captivity or allowed to roam in an enclosed stand of pines.

A few years earlier William had moved from New York to Lawrence, Kansas, where James taught at the state university. Normally James accompanied William on any long-distance travels, but this was a special case. William wouldn't be making a public appearance, and James happened to be otherwise occupied, immersed in the final stages of work on Gus Van Sant's film *Drugstore*

Cowboy, for which he—James—had written the script.

James initially contacted Roger Manley about the impending visit, since he knew Roger lived in Durham. But a prior commitment required Roger to leave town the day after William's arrival. Since I lived nearby, James wondered if I'd be willing to drive over to Durham. William would need to be picked up at his hotel and driven with Allen to the Primate Center, where a special tour had been arranged. He would also need to be entertained for a couple of days. Roger had offered the use of his house for that purpose, and as a crash pad for myself and anyone else involved.

"William is easily amused," James told me. "He likes very simple American food, and after dinner he likes to drink vodka. Cheap vodka is fine, it's all the same to him. And some good cannabis to smoke, if you can arrange it. As for company, if you could gather a small group of intelligent, younger men who would enjoy meeting William, that would be great."

And so it was that I spent a couple of days hanging out with William Burroughs and Allen Ginsberg in Durham, North Carolina, where I met several other intriguing characters in the bargain. Bill Rich, the young editor of a Kansas-based punk-rock magazine, had come along to keep Burroughs company. Weston LaBarre, the anthropologist and pioneering expert on ritual peyote use among the Plains Indians, was emeritus faculty at Duke, and an old friend of Allen. During the post-reading reception I chatted with him about psychedelics. Looking distinguished and professorial in a brown suit and a Phi Beta Kappa pin, he confided that he'd kept a vial of Sandoz mescaline in his home freezer since the 1960s.

And then there was Doctor Elwyn Simons, the Primate Center's director, and our guide for the VIP tour on the morning after Allen's reading. We spent several hours seeing the facilities and being introduced to some of the primates. William seemed particularly enamored of Poe, the aye-aye—a striking nocturnal beast who observed us warily from his special, ultraviolet-lit cell. Doctor Simons was a cheerful, informative expert who knew as much about life in Madagascar as he did about lemurs. He seemed to enjoy showing us around.

On the day after our Primate Center tour Allen had to catch a late-morning flight home to New York. Over breakfast in the hotel where he and William were both staying, he told me about his recent visit to Howard Finster's Paradise Garden with friends from Atlanta.

To take advantage of the airline discount William stayed over a second night. I drove him back to the Primate Center for another visit, and I ferried him between his hotel and Roger Manley's house, where Roger's young friend Rodney Dickens—who could've passed for one of

William's *Wild Boys*— barbecued a couple of chickens on the backyard grill.

For dinner we were joined by friends including journalists Godfrey Cheshire and Chris Redd. Afterwards William relaxed with a few drinks and many tokes on John Snow's bamboo-stick one-hitter—he said he wanted one of his own—while regaling us with stories and acerbic observations in his classic midwestern drawl.

A memorable few days, all in all. We got some terrific photos of William, Allen, and the lemurs at the Primate Center, and I interviewed William for a long article I published in the *Arts Journal* later that summer.

*

The second and last exhibition at the "John Snow Gallery"—as John was then calling his downstairs space—was a group show in November 1989, "The Issue of Censorship," held in conjunction with a regional forum on "art, censorship, and the limits of expression." These events reflected mounting concerns about the right-wing backlash against contemporary art.

I missed the forum due to obligations in Asheville, but I got a kick out of seeing "The Issue of Censorship," which was lively and feisty if predictably uneven, as it was an open-invitation theme show. Like Diana's 1988 exhibition it was fleeting, on view for only a few days, so it unfortunately came and went without critical review, by me or anyone else.

36. CLOSINGS AND CONTINUITIES

While the anti-art crusaders found new targets almost daily, another kind of cultural toll was being taken through fatal attrition. The number of AIDS-attributed deaths continued to climb steeply, as disease claimed countless victims in society's cultural sector. Too many were close friends or people I'd admired from a distance.

Ernie Mickler was only forty-eight when he met his end on November fifteenth, 1988—a sad milestone ironically coinciding with Ten Speed Press' publication of his second book, *Sinkin Spells, Hot Flashes, Fits and Cravins*. And—speaking of Robert Mapplethorpe—he died four months later with related symptoms. Among the many others fatalities of 1989 was friend and colleague Robert Lynch, pioneer art collector and the unofficial third co-curator of our 1985 visionary folk-art show. Gone at forty-one.

Every day was the Day of the Dead in the late 1980s. It was heartbreaking, but the hard times yielded rich material for surviving artists and writers. Especially in North Carolina and the Southeast, the Bible Belt's big, brassy buckle. It was an invigorating time to write about my specialty subjects, and to oversee a monthly publication focused on art in the region. From the *Arts Journal* perspective, there was no need to scramble for worthy copy and no shortage of lively, timely imagery to reproduce in our pages.

Worst of times, best of times.

*

And what, meanwhile, of Roger Manley, my Folk Art Project collaborator and fellow Raider of the Lost Art?

Roger's tracks aren't hard to follow. After his consulting position for the Jargon Society expired, he helped oversee a few related projects that were similarly ambitious. First he organized the long-awaited Annie Hooper extravaganza at North Carolina State University—a comprehensive show of Hooper's sprawling biblical tableaux, which the university's art collection had officially acquired, and an accompanying two-day symposium in the spring of 1988. I gave these events ample coverage in my first issue of the *Arts Journal*, which featured Roger's portrait of Hooper on the front cover—the one that she'd complained made her look like a spook.

The other big development in Roger's career during those years was the North Carolina Museum of Art's 1989 exhibition "Signs and Wonders: Outsider Art Inside North Carolina," which he assembled with the museum's in-house curator David Steel. Roger's photographs, essay, and artists' biographies in the accompanying catalog distilled more than a decade's worth of his research, and the show included works by several artists from our

"Southern Visionary Folk Artists" exhibition. It opened in Raleigh that summer and would travel to a couple of other in-state museums during the following year. It deserved to be far more widely seen.

As for the Jargon Society, founder Jonathan Williams continued to direct the maverick publishing house from his dual headquarters in Scaly Mountain, North Carolina, and Cumbria, England, with financial oversight provided by Whitney Jones and Thorns Craven in Winston-Salem, and assorted board members in their scattered locales. After *White Trash Cooking* and *St. EOM in the Land of Pasaquan* Jargon returned to its original mission, publishing new books of poetry by James Broughton, Simon Cutts, and Joel Oppenheimer. (I wrote about the Oppenheimer book in the *Arts Journal*.) During the same year, 1988, the press also issued one of its outstanding "picture books," as Jonathan called them—*Bill Anthony's Greatest Hits*, a selection of the artist's self-described bad drawings.

In 1989 Jonathan edited a Jargon festschrift honoring longtime patron and Jargon board member Don Anderson on his seventieth birthday (*DBA at 70*). And Jargon entered its fifth decade with new volumes by Peyton Houston, Richard Emil Braun, and Paul Metcalf (whose 1991 book *Araminta and the Coyotes* features a cover painting by self-taught visionary artist Mary T. Smith).

Jonathan's *Big Book of Southern Folk Art*, referenced multiple times here, wouldn't be published until long after his death. In 2019 it appeared under the title *Walks to the Paradise Garden: A Low-down Southern Odyssey* (Institute 193).

What about R.E.M.? "America's Best Rock & Roll Band," according to the December 1987 issue of *Rolling Stone.*

The Jargon benefit concert I envisioned never materialized, but Michael Stipe sometimes spontaneously promoted our Folk Art Project from the stage during the band's shows in the late '80s. He also incorporated some of his own photographs of visionary folk art and artists into their increasingly elaborate visual backdrops.

How many of the fans caught these references, or went home and researched them? How many ordered a Jargon book or contributed a few dollars to the cause? Probably none. Still, I always got a kick out of seeing one of Leroy Person's tiny peafowl sculptures or Saint EOM's painted-concrete mandalas enlarged to billboard scale behind the band, and hearing Jargon's name uttered by an international rock star, amplified into the ears of a few thousand boys and girls in a huge arena.

*

Abbeville Press published *Howard Finster, Stranger from Another World* in the summer of 1989, coinciding with the release of John Turner's book *Howard Finster, Man of Visions* by Alfred Knopf. It would have been hard to argue that the simultaneous publication harmed any of the parties involved. As for Finster, his popularity was undoubtedly boosted further by the two books. He'd already become an American icon, as famous as Allen Ginsberg.

By that time I'd been writing a weekly art column for the *Winston-Salem Journal* and editing the *Arts Journal* for a little more than a year. I'll skip the grueling details, but my arrangement with the *AJ* was wearing thin. It would finally end under strained circumstances in the summer of 1990. Still burdened with thousands of dollars in debt, the *Arts Journal* would struggle along for another year through the valiant efforts of temporary editors and fill-ins, but the board would throw in the towel and shut it down in 1991, presumably with some reluctance.

Like so much else, that milestone takes place in a future beyond the scope of this little recollection.

Tom Patterson, 1986. Photo by Roger Manley.

TOM PATTERSON is writer, editor, and independent curator based in North Carolina. His books include *St. EOM in the Land of Pasaquan* (Jargon Society, 1987; University of Georgia Press, 2018), *Howard Finster, Stranger from Another World* (Abbeville Press, 1989), and *The Tom Patterson Years: Cultural Adventures of a Fledgling Scribe* (Hiding Press, 2021). His writings have appeared in *afterimage*, *American Crafts, Aperture, ARTnews, Art Papers, BOMB, Folk Art*, and *New Art Examiner*. A frequent, longtime contributor to *Raw Vision*, the London-based international outsider-art journal, he is also a former editor of North Carolina's *Arts Journal* (1988-1990), and a former visual-art columnist for the *Charlotte Observer* (1992-1998) and the *Winston-Salem Journal* (1988-2022). He has curated exhibitions for the American Visionary Art Museum, the Southeastern Center for Contemporary Art, and the College of Charleston's Halsey Institute for Contemporary Art, among other visual-art institutions.

www.ingramcontent.com/pod-product-compliance
Lightning Source LLC
Chambersburg PA
CBHW011214120626
46545CB00008B/2986